VARIATIONS

BY JAMES HUNEKER

MEZZOTINTS IN MODERN MUSIC (1899)

CHOPIN: THE MAN AND HIS MUSIC (1900)

MELOMANIACS (1902)

OVERTONES (1904)

ICONOCLASTS: A BOOK OF DRAMATISTS (1905)

VISIONARIES (1905)

EGOISTS: A BOOK OF SUPERMEN (1909)

PROMENADES OF AN IMPRESSIONIST (1910)

FRANZ LISZT. ILLUSTRATED (1911)

THE PATHOS OF DISTANCE (1912)

NEW COSMOPOLIS (1915)

IVORY APES AND PEACOCKS (1915)

UNICORNS (1917)

BEDOUINS (1920)

STEEPLEJACK. TWO VOLUMES (1920)

VARIATIONS (1921)

CHARLES SCRIBNER'S SONS

VARIATIONS

BY

JAMES HUNEKER

—

NEW YORK

CHARLES SCRIBNER'S SONS

1922

PUBLISHER'S NOTE

Mr. Huneker's literary career was at its flood when ended by his sudden and unlooked for death. He was perhaps our only, certainly our chief, literary journalist, and his instructive, penetrating, and, above all, entertaining criticism in the field of what he liked to call the Seven Arts was almost always first seen in the periodical press, daily or weekly. Afterward it was sifted and the residue abridged or expanded, burnished or simplified, in its assimilation into appropriate permanent style and stuff. Needless to say it lost none of its brilliance in the process which was always minimized by having been largely forestalled, as it were, in the original composition. The result was not so much merely eminent as literally unique. His books have not only no rivals but no competitors. Alone among American belletristic writers he followed in the French journalistic-literary tradition, illustrated and rendered illustrious by the practice of a long and shining roll of littérateurs. Such a practice tends of itself to popularize its product by inevitably keeping the larger public more or less in mind and therefore eschewing professional pedantries. The element of personality acquires prominence as in conversation. Style itself becomes conversational. Huneker is as familiar in address as if he were not often erudite in material. He establishes first of all, however imperceptibly, his relations with his reader. Whatever the effect, it is devoid of dulness, and accordingly the interest

v

of his writing is incontestable even when its value is indeterminate.

Composed of essays written since the publication of his last book — Bedouins — though of necessity lacking the advantage of his personal selection and supervision, Variations is a worthy companion of its shelf-full of predecessors in its possession of these qualities. Aptly named, it presents perhaps better than any of them a wide-reaching diversity of æsthetic material for the consideration, the illumination, and — pre-eminently — the entertainment of the cultivated. Perhaps, too, it shows a maturer treatment, a mellower temper without a whit less energy, and a greater opulence than ever of the author's stored acquisitions and spontaneous, even exhilarated, exposition of them. And here and there amid the wealth of literary and æsthetic miscellany which he displays and expounds one comes, with greater frequency than ever, upon memorable crystallizations of experience in the contemplation of these matters. Such truths, too, he exemplifies as well as formulates. No one ever, for instance, credited more completely his own maxim: "There is no disputing tastes — with the tasteless," or conformed more cordially to his own injunction: "Write only for the young. The old will not heed you, being weary of the pother of life and art." There was nothing, however, of which *he* was less weary, as this his last volume copiously attests, and the explanation, of course, is his unimpaired youthfulness of mind and spirit.

CONTENTS

CONTENTS

VARIATIONS

VARIOUS

COLERIDGE quotes Sir Joshua Reynolds as declaring that: "The greatest man is he who forms the taste of a nation; the next greatest is he who corrupts it." It is an elastic epigram and not unlike the rule which is poor because it won't work both ways. All master reformers, heretics, and rebels at first were great corrupters. "Corruption," so-called, is a prime factor in their propaganda. Buddha, Jesus, and Moses; Arius and Aristophanes, Mohammed and Napoleon, Paul and Augustine, Luther and Calvin, Voltaire and Rousseau, Darwin and Newman, Liszt and Wagner, Kant and Schopenhauer — here are a few names of men who undermined the current beliefs and practices of their epoch, whether for good or for evil. Rousseau has been accused by Pierre Lasserre as being the greatest corrupter in modern history; yet his name will always be associated with the Constitution of the United States of America. Tom Paine has been called a "dirty little atheist," but he wrote The Rights of Man. In prose of unequalled force and limpidity Pascal denounced the Jesuits as corrupters of youth — poor, persecuted Jesuits, who were the "Yellow Peril" of that time. Nevertheless, Dr. Georg Brandes, an "intellectual" and a philosophic anarch, wrote to Friedrich Nietzsche: "I, too, love Pascal. But even as a young man I was on the side of the Jesuits against Pascal. Wise men, it was they who were right; he did not understand them; but they understood him and . . . they published his Provincial Letters with notes. The best edition is that of the Jesuits."

Were not Titian, Rubens, and Rembrandt the three unspeakable devils of painting for William Blake? Loosely speaking, then, it doesn't much matter whether we consider a great man as either a regenerator or a corrupter. It all depends on your critical angle of vision. Taine called Napoleon a bandit, notwithstanding the idolatries of his contemporaries. Nor does the case of Nietzsche differ much from that of his philosophic forerunners. He scolded Schopenhauer, although he borrowed his dialectic tools, as he later mocked at the sincerest friendship of his solitary life—his love for Richard Wagner. We know that the most "objective" — comical old categories, "objective" and "subjective" — philosophies are tinged by the temperaments of their makers; perhaps the chief characteristic of philosophers is their unphilosophic contempt for fellow-thinkers. This trait Schopenhauer displayed when he abused Hegel & Co., Berlin, Ltd. Nietzsche attacked Wagner after writing that lucid and comprehensive study of him, Richard Wagner and Baireuth. Wagner was a bitter polemist and didn't spare Meyerbeer and other operatic trusts. He was an amateur philosopher, his rickety system adorned with plumes borrowed from Feuerbach, Schelling, and Schopenhauer. But Arthur Schopenhauer was endowed with a more powerful, more original intellect than either Wagner or Nietzsche. He "corrupted" both, though it may be admitted that their intellectual and artistic soil was primed for just such corruption. And Schopenhauer, gay old misogynist, was materialist enough to echo an epigram attributed to Fontenelle: "To be happy a man must have a good stomach and a wicked heart." In other words, if your stomach is sound your soul will take care of itself. All Hobbes, Destutt de Tracy, Cabanis, Helvétius, and Condillac are in that phrase.

But it is not my intention to stray among the pleasant groves of speculation, taking an occasional potshot at the strange fauna of metaphysic or admiring its many-colored flora. Some one wrote asking me if Manette Salomon, by de Goncourt — the brothers Edmond and Jules, — had been translated into English; also if it were the only fiction about art and artists. I can't say yes or no as to the translation; if it is not, it should be; but it is safe to say that Manette is the best novel dealing entirely with paint and painters that I know of. Fiction about art and artists is rare; that is, good fiction, not the stuff daily ground out by publishing mills for the gallery gods. A classic example in American literature is The Marble Faun, by Hawthorne. Romola, by George Eliot, is atmospheric with Florentine art and the genius of place. However, it is to the French that we must go for such literature, Manette being a notable example. It depicts the spiritual and physical decadence of a splendid painting talent, Coriolis, and contains veracious pictures of the pre-impressionist days in Paris. Balzac in the Unknown Masterpiece has left a model. His Frenhofer is the first of the impressionists withal, a fumbler of genius. In both Daudet and de Maupassant there are stories clustered about the artistic guild. Strong as Death, by de Maupassant, is long enough to be called a novel (roman), though it is but an expanded episode, and a mighty interesting one, even a touching one, for the usually impassive Guy. Daudet described a Paris Salon on varnishing day in his accustomed facile, febrile style; but it stems from Goncourt and Zola. Zola's His Masterpiece (L'Œuvre) is one of his best-written books. It was said to be a favorite of his, and it justifies his taste. The much-belauded fifth chapter is a faithful transcription of the first Salon of Rejected Painters (Salon des refusés) at Paris in 1863. Napoleon III, after social and political pressure had been brought to bear on him, had consented to a special Salon within the official Salon at the Palais de l'Industrie, where the rejected work of the young lunatics who wished to paint purple turkeys, vermilion water, and black sunsets would be harbored. Ivory hallucinations and girls with carmilion-colored eyes were not barred. It is an

4

enormously clever book, this chiefly deriving from Manette Salomon and Balzac's Frenhofer. Claude Lantier is said to be the portrait of Paul Cézanne, a schoolmate and friend of Zola at Aix-en-Provence. When I made the trip from Marseilles to Aix Cézanne still lived, but I had been warned not to mention the name of Zola, who shows Cézanne in this novel as an impotent groper after impossible ideals. The irritable Paul would go into spasms of rage when Zola was referred to in his presence. Imbecile, traitor, charlatan! These were sample expressions. A reading of L'Œuvre at once convinces you that the artistic procedures of Claude Lantier and Paul Cézanne are diametrically different. Claude failed and hanged himself. There are contemporary critics who consider Cézanne the greatest master of the impressionist group. But the struggle for artistic veracity on the part of Zola's sorry hero is not unlike the case of Manet. The Breakfast on the Grass, described by Zola, was actually the title and the subject of a Manet canvas that had scandalized Paris at this period. The fantastic idea of nude females at an al fresco banquet upon the grass, while the other figures were clothed and in their right mind — all this was too much for a purblind public and hostile critics; although there are many examples in Italian renaissance painting of the same style of composition. The picture became notorious. Manet, like Richard Wagner, knew the uses of advertising.

VARIATIONS

Whistler's remarks about the Irish critic, especially after the Eden litigation, were, so it is reported, not "fit to print."

In Spring Days, the first volume of Mr. Moore's trilogy — A Modern Lover and Mike Fletcher are the other two — we are shown a young painter who thinks more of petticoats than paint. Mike Fletcher, the most virile and, for some of us, the quintessence of Moore, has its share of paint talk. In A Modern Lover the hero is an artist who succeeds in the fashionable world by painting pretty, artificial portraits, thereby winning wealth, popular applause, and official approbation. He also makes love in a fascinating fashion — the secret of his mundane success. This same Lewis Seymour lives and paints modish London beauties in rose color. He may be found in Paris and New York. He is a type. The sitter for this portrait is said to have been Sir Frederick Leighton, a statement I accept on its face value, and one that Mr. Moore would probably vehemently deny. But his irony must have entered the souls of a hundred celebrated humbugs; that is, if they had souls to boast. A Modern Lover, despite the rewriting and consequent defacement of the original design, is distinctly a painter's novel and the best of its kind, were it not that subsequently the novelist wrote a masterpiece, Mildred Lawson, to be found in the volume entitled Celibates — a Balzacian title, by the way. Masterly in analysis and description,

8

this story chiefly deals with art. Mildred, a selfish English girl without heart, soul, or talent, studies in the Julian atelier and goes to Fontainebleau during the summer vacation. Naturally, no one has ever described the Forest better than Flaubert in Sentimental Education; Flaubert, who wrote better than any one else save Balzac. In this great canvas of Parisian life there are marvellous evocations. There is a semi-burlesque painter, Pellerin, who first reads all the literature of æsthetics before he draws a line, and poses his sitters à la Van Dyck, Rubens, Gainsborough, or Titian; in a word, the man of precedent. De Goncourt, too, has excelled in his impressions of the Forest and its painters; in particular, François Millet.

It is only just to Mr. Moore to say that you can't find Mildred Lawson in Flaubert or de Goncourt; no, not even in Balzac, whose work is the very matrix of modern fiction. She is her own cruel, perverse, Moorovian self, and she lives here or London or in the Philippines. Elsewhere I have classed her as one of the most disagreeable heroines in fiction, an inky sister of Hedda Gabler and Undine Spragg (in Edith Wharton's Custom of the Country).

All the one-time novel theories of "plein air" impressionism are discussed in Zola's His Masterpiece, yet the work as a whole lacks the fine-fibred style and clairvoyance of Manette Salomon; that breviary for painters which in 1867 anticipated the experimentings, the discoveries, and the practice of the naturalistic and impressionist groups, running the gamut from Manet, Monet, to Cézanne, Maufra, and Paul Gauguin. The book is crowded with verbal pictures of art students, atelier and open-air life; painting was still one of the romantic arts when de Goncourt wrote. No such psychological manual of the painter has appeared, before or since, Manette Salomon. The celibate bias of the brothers is revealed in the leading motive — oh, that musty, fusty melodramatic idea — which is the degradation of a man's artistic ideals because of the woman — Manette, his model — he marries. It was Goncourt who introduced Japanese art to Europe; the brothers were friends of the late M. Bing, a pioneer collector in Paris. And they foresaw the future of fiction as well as painting.

HOW NOT TO BE A GENIUS

How not to be a genius nowadays is as difficult as it is to believe in prohibition. Every other man and woman you meet on the sidewalks of life is a genius; at least they admit it, or their disciples say they are. People with mere talent are becoming rare. If you happen to write a best seller you are acclaimed a genius. And when you think it over, a man who can sell a million copies of a book compounded of sentimental slush and slimy piety must be a genius. What else is he? An artistic writer? No. Respectable? Yes. In Carlyle's times a person was considered respectable if he owned a gig; he was called a gigman. To-day it is the motor-car that is the symbol of financial well-being. Carlyle had much fun with his gigman. What would he write about those egregious humans who starve themselves and their families in order to sport about the highways in a mortgaged motor? Popularity may be for dolls, declared Emerson, but it's a mighty asset when all the world is a doll. Even the old Carlyle definition was thrown out of court by Herbert Spencer, himself a prize specimen of one who possessed an infinite capacity for taking pains in his work. Nevertheless, industry is not necessarily an indication of genius, although elbow-grease has been an underrated factor in the case. The truth is that there are no royal paths to Parnassus.

In 1857 Dr. Morel published his Traité des Dégénérescences, and gave modern psychiatry its initial springboard. Then Guerensen pronounced genius a disease of the nerves, and the floodgates of madcap theories were wide opened. We learned much from Magnan, Ribot, the brothers Janet, Maudsley, Esquinol, and Charcot. After their psychological plumber work genius became a dangerous profession. You were likely to be either a madman or a criminal, and such piffling busybodies as Lombroso and Nordau tracked you to your lair, measured your ears, the cut of your nose and a glance of the eye, Reginald! (Surely Beau Brummel was a clothes maniac.)

Luckily for the world, genius is still a scarce product, and the charlatan theories were laughed off the map when Nordau wrote his partly amusing and wholly ridiculous book on Degeneration. The late William James walloped him into silence. But the vulgar error persists in the mind of the half-baked of culture. Like Mahomet's coffin, it hangs suspended 'twixt earth and heaven. It bobs up in the so-called new school of Freudian psychoanalysis, which exploits to the reductio ad absurdum the von Hartmann theory of the subliminal consciousness, with a little spice of soothsaying and dreambook twaddle thrown in to lend an air of novelty.

HOW NOT TO BE A GENIUS

We learn from Dr. Freud that dreams are the result of unfulfilled desires — which may mean anything — that authors unconsciously reveal themselves in their writings. What an astounding discovery! Important if true. O la belle histoire! Cut out the erotic element in this "new" theory and the world would pass it by. Who would read Leaves of Grass for its "poetry" if such chaste, odoriferous "poems" as The Woman Who Waits for Me were absent?

Genius is a word that has fallen into disrepute because of its being bandied about so freely by our makers of fiction. That burlesque of a raw-head-and-bloody-bones, Strickland, the alleged painter in Somerset Maugham's melodramatic "shocker," The Moon and Sixpence, is a case in point. The clever author expects his readers to believe that a staid business man is transformed into a great painter at the age of forty. To be sure, Strickland was what the French call a "Sunday painter," one who potters with color tubes and canvas every seventh day, yet is supposed to accomplish what such men of genius as Degas, Manet, Millet, couldn't in protracted daily toil. And the innocent public swallows such fairy-tales because it believes in miracles. You may be sure of one thing — no one in the history of the Seven Arts has mastered his material save in the sweat of his brow. Works and days. You can't change your psychology overnight. Mr. Maugham suggested Paul Gauguin, the painter of South Seas landscapes, rich in color, decoration and arabesques. But Gauguin was a real genius. Augustus John too has been dragged in. Ridiculous! We mention Strickland because he seems to embody the popular notion of genius. A bolt from the blue, and a stupid Philistine becomes in a trice a scarecrow painter. No, he won't do, any more than Theodore Dreiser's The Genius will serve as a portrait of one. In Shakespeare you are jostled by genius, but, then, the poet was a genius of geniuses. He englobed all forms of genius.

But is genius a disease, like the tenor voice, or the pearl in a mollusk? It is, we know, a gift that seldom brings happiness to its possessor. Either it is unmercifully flouted, or else unrecognized, and no two persons agree as to its specific quality. There is in Poland a poet-novelist-playwright who bears a name that sounds like an unconquered Polish fortress. He is called Stanislaw Przybyszewski, and when his story, Homo Sapiens, was translated and published here the unhappy man was heartily hated by all proofreaders and compositors. Do you wonder? Possibly that dislike was a factor in the suppression of the book, which wasn't a whit less moral in its implications than the Re-creation of William J. Bryan Kent. Stanislaw — we mercifully omit the full name — has wisely written of genius and has illustrated it in his exceedingly vivid personal career. Readers of Strindberg's Inferno, which contains in compression more tortures than Dante's epic, a sort of pemmican hell, need hardly be reminded that the rival to the Swedish dramatist's affections is Stanislaw P. in the guise of a pianist who plays with overwhelming power and pathos the F sharp minor polonaise of Chopin. That is the way the super-subtle Pole courted one of Strindberg's lady-loves; it may have been a matrimonial rib, but that is a mere detail.

Stanislaw asserts in his brochure, Chopin and Nietzsche, that physicians do not busy themselves enough with history; if they did they would recognize that "decadence" has always existed; that it is not decadence at all, but only a phase of development quite as important as normality; normality is stupidity, decadence is genius. Is there, he demands, a more notable case of the abnormal than the apostle of Protestantism, Martin Luther? We are all children of Satan, he cries. Those rare men who for the sake of their ideals sacrifice the lives and happiness of thousands, such as Alexander or Napoleon — there are more modern instances, if we cared to mention them; or those who dispel the dreams of youth, Socrates and Schopenhauer; or those who venture into the depths of sin — because sin has depth — Poe, Baudelaire, Rops; and those who love pain for the sake of pain and ascend the Golgotha of mankind, Chopin, Schumann, Nietzsche — of such material is genius compounded. Satan is the first philosopher, the first Anarchist, and pain is the foundation of all art and, with Satan, the father of illusions. I quote these luminous reflections to prove how easy it is to twist a theory so as to suit one's own point of view. The decadence theory is nonsense. I may only refer you to Havelock Ellis's masterly volume of critical essays, entitled Affirmations, for a concise refutation of the heresy; and equally fallacious is the contention of the Polish writer that the normal always spells stupidity. The reverse is often the case. Coleridge, you may remember, disputed, in his Biographia Literaria, that antique sarcasm of Horace, the "genus irritabile vatum." He wrote: "The men of the greatest genius, as far as we can judge from their own works or from the accounts of their contemporaries, appeared to have been of calm and tranquil temper in all that related to themselves." Coleridge gives examples to uphold this belief. Taine has written in his history of English literature of the sane genius among such old chaps as Rabelais, Montaigne, Shakespeare, and Goethe, all of whom performed prodigies of labor. No neurasthenia hampered their literary invention. Yet Shakespeare created Hamlet, the incarnation of a disordered will and a poetic soul astray.

Schopenhauer has adequately dealt with the theme and with more conviction-breeding results than many of the later explorers in this field, at his time a field outside of the biological laboratory. He finds that "talent is versatile and betrays more acuteness of discursive than intuitive knowledge." The genius beholds another world because he has a profounder conception of the world which lies before us all, inasmuch as it presents itself with more objectivity and distinctness than it does to less favored mortals. Myriad-minded Goethe summed up the question in a memorable phrase. "Genius is incommensurable," he told Eckermann when discussing Faust. Mozart confessed that music came to him without his volition. So-called secondary selves exist in the subliminal mind, and in certain circumstances may usurp the reign of the primary self for varying periods of time, just as a saint and sinner may inhabit one soul. The old theologians spoke of guardian angels and angels of evil. Some see God in an ecstatic vision and others peer into the fiery pit of hell with morose delectation. Don't worry about this moral dichotomy. It's only your various selves at war. When the dissociation becomes a half-dozen split-up personalities struggling for mastery then it is time to consult a psychiatrist. That way lies the madhouse. But we are all of us the victims of our cells.

A genius is a superman — a man, according to Dr. Jacobson (see his Possible Clues to the Nature of Genius), plus a secondary personality, his genius not residing in the primary self but in his secondary personality. In the one case we have the spiritualistic medium — low mentality, irresponsible secondary personality; in the other case we have genius — high mentality, super-rational secondary personality. It might be well to remember this fact just now when a wave of debasing superstition is rising everywhere, of which the mildest symptom is the Ouija-board and other clotted nonsense; the gravest symptoms, devil-worship and alleged communication with spirits; after all cataclysmic events, war, pestilence, earthquake, the prolonged nerve-tension causes "new" religions, witchcraft, healers, and prophets of evil to flourish like toadstools in a damp, dank cellar. Mock-turtle mysticism and ineffable silliness. It is not the denial of such so-called "phenomena" that concerns us, for there are numberless unexplained mysteries in nature; all occult research is not hocus-pocus; but it is the interpretation, divine or diabolic, of these happenings to which sensible thinkers object. Bateson, quoted by Dr. Jacobson, "conceives of evolution and life as an unpacking of an original complex." Here we are knocking at the transcendental gates of the Fourth Spatial Dimension. Life is an uncoiling. Humanity is a watch-spring of the infinite. Our existence is the progress of a spiritual tapeworm. Death is the grand vermifuge. Nevertheless, genius is a shy bird. Spear him and put him under the microscope. But first catch your fish. And that is always difficult.

Man has chartered the globe, but, probably by reason of an almost ineradicable superstitious timidity, has left the human soul an undiscovered country, or, at least, but partially explored. Genius, whether manifesting its power in the arts or in the sciences, is the worthiest theme for the philosopher; not reactionary metaphysicians like Bergson, weavers of verbal dreams, spinners of futile cobweb systems; but the biologist, psychiatrist, the practical scientist, for whom the visible as well as the invisible worlds exist. "I breathe, therefore I live," said, in effect, William James. (Essays in Radical Empiricism.) The mind of man has ever been a house divided in itself. Yet it is a consolation to know that our several subliminal personalities may be the cause of our conflicting thoughts. (The late Prof. Muensterburg declared that such a thing as subconsciousness did not exist.) In Faust we read of two spirits that abide in our breast, also the spirit that denied. Mephisto then may be only our second personality. However, we haven't answered the question posed at the beginning of this Sunday morning ramble through the tangled forest of minor speculation — how not to be a genius. The answer is as easy as lying — never work!

THE RECANTATIONS OF GEORGE MOORE

I HAD intended writing of the tragic Chopin to-day, but George Moore supervened; he and Atlantic City — an odd combination. Man cannot live in music alone, and when Maurice Speiser met me on the boardwalk and lent me his copy of Avowals (numbered eighty and privately printed for subscribers), I shooed Chopin to the backyard of my consciousness and proceeded to reread Mr. Moore. I say reread because much of the subject-matter in this new, bulky volume saw the light of publication years ago in various English and at least one American periodical: Lippincotts', the Fortnightly, et al. Still, it is, all of it, worthwhile, notwithstanding the fact the old nurse of the County Mayo author wouldn't have blushed at a line therein. Why the book was published as "wicked" by implication is difficult to discover. It should be given to the world at large, after several minor excisions. The one gay anecdote is related in France, and it is so mildly diverting that it will bear repeating here. An eccentric nobleman adorns himself with peacock's feathers for the edification of his peahens! Yet people subscribe for the pleasure of such innocent foolery. By all means, let us have Avowals naked and unashamed. Only good Moorovians will endure its leagues of technical literary criticism. The Story Teller's Holiday of last year was another kind of a book. Rather blistering than elevating. But amusing always.

There was a time when Mr. Moore was content to be called the Irish Flaubert; nowadays he is evidently after the title of the Celtic Casanova, though hardly in these new avowals. They will never rank in interest with Memoirs of My Dead Life; or, indeed, with his Hail and Farewell Trilogy. For one thing, printed dialogue makes slow reading, even when the prose is the incomparable prose of Walter Savage Landor. The opening chapters are devoted to discussions, purely academic, between Edmund Gosse and George Moore. English prose narrative is the weakest part of English literature — a paradoxical contention. Mr. Gosse puts up a good fight, but is pulverized by his opponent, who leaves him gasping on a balcony wrapped in a shawl, feebly expostulating. The Moore dialectic is fairly familiar to his admirers. It is one-third lack of logic and two-thirds persuasion and browbeating. Need I add that the persuasiveness is not wholly divested of a certain veiled Donnybrookishness? Mr. Moore goes for the hated Sassenach, and only those Englishmen who seem to resemble him are treated with consideration; the Rev. Laurence Sterne, whose wheedling prose style is admirably wedded to his prurient themes ("Are you Jewish or ticklish?" he was asked by a critic long ago), is praiseworthy in the eyes of our critic.

I should have preferred to pose as an adversary to Mr. Moore the redoubtable Prof. George Saintsbury, who with a Sam Johnson bluffness would have smashed the Irishman's arguments at the very first throw out of the box. No doubt about that. Mr. Moore admits the genius of Landor, Pater, Lamb, De Quincey, in the essay form; but it is fiction narrative he centres upon, and despite De Foe, Fielding, Jane Austen, not to speak of Dickens, Thackeray and Meredith, he finds no good has come forth from that British Nazareth. Of the exquisite prose patterns which Cardinal Newman has woven for us he speaks no word; elsewhere, years past, he has expressed his dislike of Newman's flowing style; the "style coulant" abhorred of Charles Baudelaire, especially when it issued from the pen of George Sand. Yet Mr. Moore's Keltic prose (spell it with a K, Samivel!) is like Newman's in so far as both are subtle, sensitive, and rippling; both avoid dynamic contrasts, both persuade rather than assault. And there is a suspicion of the serpentine in the writings of both men. The spiral prose of The Brook Kerith is a case in point. Can't you see that minotaur of English literary criticism — or should I say Torquemada? — George Saintsbury frowning and thundering on Mr. Moore, and quoting

from his History of English Prose-Rhythms!
A battle of the bookmen, indeed.

The recantations of George Moore become
increasingly numerous with the passage of the
years. I had expected the inclusion in Avowals
of his top-notch in criticism, not dealing with
the plastic arts — naturally his stronghold — a
criticism that appeared about twenty years
ago in *Cosmopolis*, an international magazine
edited, if I remember aright, by Lady Randolph
Churchill. Far finer than his study of Zola is
this study of Flaubert's Sentimental Education,
entitled A Tragic Novel, the tragedy of drab,
commonplace living, not that of high heroics
or tragic and romantic gestures. But Mr. Moore
violently repudiates his Flaubert worship and
explains why he doesn't reprint the splendid
pages of that particular criticism. Flaubert, it
seems, is not a novelist, only a satirist — he
says something of the same sort earlier concerning George Meredith — and he places him
far below Balzac as a creator of character, below Turgénieff as a teller of tales; he even de-
cries his style — the sanity, simplicity, which,
allied to its sonorous harmonies, is one of the
most fascinating in French literature. I fancy
Mr. Moore suffered from the revulsion which
often attacks critical pioneers; as soon as the
public, wooed or banged into submission by the
critic, begins to admire them the critic moves
on; his object accomplished, newer idols must
be sought, fresher victories achieved; the old

idol is again become a block of wood. Mr.
Saintsbury fought for Baudelaire and Flaubert
before George Moore; nevertheless, Mr. Moore
was the first English-writing novelist who
adopted Flaubert's methods; recall Untilled
Fields and Evelyn Inness — the manner, of
course, not the matter. And there is Swinburne, who after extravagantly praising Walt
Whitman violently repudiated the Camden
"bard," later inventing the word "Whitmaniac"
to signify his contempt for Walt's comical yawp-
ing. In humbler fashion I may give as an
example of this critical dog-in-the-manger attitude my own case. In 1877 I went as a lad to
visit Walt across the Delaware River from my
home, and from him received the kiss of peace
and went away with the glowing brow of the
neophyte. I became an ardent Whitmaniac
in my teens, and for two decades or more I wrote
of W. W. as if he were really a great poet. I
can't read him now, nor can I read the effusions
of his followers. He has been a disruptive force,
still is one; to imitate his "poetry" is so easy
that an entire new school of lads and lassies
are murdering English prosody and filling the
urn with their lascivious caterwaulings. Walt
is to blame. He did it first in his Children of
Adam.

Flaubert is not the only writer from whom
Mr. Moore has seceded. Being a peculiarly
susceptible Celt, he is always changing his
opinions, which is a legitimate function of the

male as well as the female intellect. At one epoch Dublin never knew when beginning a fresh day whether her favorite son was a Catholic or a Protestant. It was like a barometrical puzzle. He recanted his Catholicism — decanted might be a better word — and he changed his mind every morning about his best friend, the poet, William Yeats. The New Irish movement was to be George Moore or it was to be nothing. Finally John Millington Synge appeared, and the movement, luckily enough, became Synge. Being dead, this master is spared from the scarifications to which Moore subjected Yeats, Edward Martyn, and Lady Gregory. Ireland is no longer Erin go bragh! and the Lord knows what he thinks of Sinn Fein. In fact, since Ireland did not appreciate the genius of George Moore, he abandons Ireland — as he abandoned England during the Boer Rebellion. We hear no more of Douglas Hyde or the revival of Erse — says the Shan Van Vocht!

He sharply criticised Jane Austen and women writers generally in articles published in the *North American Review*, but in Avowals Jane is given her just dues, which is well. George Eliot and the Brontës he won't have. He rightfully rates Tolstoy and his absence of true spirituality. The great Russian writer is not a prober of the human soul, despite the accepted belief to the contrary; that is, he doesn't deeply probe. His rendering of reality borders on hallucination. Simply prodigious is his mastery of realism.

Yet Dostoievsky is the profounder man of the pen. He lived and suffered the life that Tolstoy only wrote about but never experienced. His novels, tedious, explosive, tumultuous, may be the "psychological mole-runs" of Turgénieff's dictum; nevertheless they are aglow with vitality, palpitating with pity for the downtrodden and humiliated, and pullulating with humanity. Dostoievsky, an essentially morbid man, as was Nietzsche, by reason of this very deviation from normality, was enabled to sink his plummet into the darkest recesses of the soul. His self-cruelty had a sadistic tinge. But he is the real psychologist, not Tolstoy. Deploring Tolstoy's dodging of psychological issues — for his religion was of the old intolerant order and he was suffering from an excess of moralic acid in the blood, which finally killed his art — Mr. Moore yet refuses to give Dostoievsky a truly exalted position. He better likes Turgénieff, nor need we quarrel with him on this score. Turgénieff represents the almost perfect artist, blithe, Greek, charming, while his rival, a Prometheus of the inkpot, groans in travail as he shows us his wounded soul. In the Confessions of a Young Man the author speaks of Dostoievsky as "Gaboriau with psychological sauce." When he wrote an introduction to a translation of Poor Folk he had evidently seen a great light. But in Avowals he is back in the Gaboriau trenches.

A more definite recantation is his present

view of Tolstoy. The first avowals, in periodical form, saw him a worshipper at the shrine. I well remember his essay, Since the Elizabethans, and its contemptuous comparison of Tolstoy and Thackeray. English fiction, he said, in effect, never dives below the surface; it is an affair of decoration, never of depth. Well and good. Tolstoy, like Balzac, has no counterpart in English literature, Mr. Moore says, and maintains his argument with admirable examples. Musical analogies are employed. Verdi or Donizetti, never the passionately profound harmonies of Wagner, are overheard in English fiction. With a sense of relief I find that Mr. Moore is still faithful to Walter Pater. The best pages in the volume are those in which he describes the art and personality of the shy, complex author of Marius. It may be remembered, his eulogy of Marius in the early confessions. From this faith he has never swerved. Of Henry James he was not an admirer. He seems not to have gone further than The Portrait of a Lady. He encountered Mr. James at the home of the Robinson girls, Mary and Mabel. Here is a portrait of our famous countryman: "And these thoughts drew my eyes to the round head, already going bald, to the small, dark eyes, closely set, and to the great expanse of closely shaven face. His legs were short, and his hands and feet large, and he sat portentously in his chair, speaking with some hesitation and great care, anxious that every sentence, or if not all, at least every

third or fourth, should send forth a beam of
humor." Apart from the fact that the eyes of
Henry James were not small, but large and
heavy lidded, eyes in which were pictured an
entire social world, his description is not without
a certain malicious verisimilitude. The two men
were, naturally enough, antipathetic to each
other. Mr. James failed to recognize the great-
ness of Esther Waters, and Mr. Moore hated
humor. He objurgates humor in a writer. Yet
he is, consciously or unconsciously, humorous.
And what a bon mot was his summing up of
Bernard Shaw as being only the "funny man in
a boarding house." Perhaps. But at the time
that boarding house comprised Europe and
America.

Moore and Whistler were always clawing and
scratching. Both feline, both tenors, and pos-
sessing the tenor temperament, how could they
be expected to sing in amiable ensemble?
Moore relates that James the Butterfly presented him with a copy of his Ten o'Clock,
inscribed: "To George Moore — for furtive
reading," which is the epitome of irony. But
George never began to repeat the epigrams
of "Jemmy," as did Jemmy those of Oscar
Wilde. Whistler, according to friends who
knew, would sit up half the night manufacturing
witticisms. It was to himself, not to Oscar,
that he should have applied the remark: "But
you will, Oscar, you will." The Irishman was
as spontaneous in his wit as the American con-

stipated. However, "furtive reading" is distinctly good. George Moore paid off his score in his Modern Painting when he wrote of Whistler that if he had been fifty pounds heavier he might have painted as well as Velasquez. And weight and substance are precisely the qualities lacking in the Whistlerian canvases, which are becoming more attenuated, more ghostly as the years wear on. If it were not for the etchings the next generation would have cause for wonderment over the exaggerated praise bestowed upon a painter whose originality principally derives from his Paris friend, Fantin-Latour, and from the Japanese.

But Avowals is good fun. It should be placed on the general market. It's too decent to be locked away in the "enfer" of a bibliophile. Apropos of nothing, did you hear George Moore on the League of Nations? He is convinced enough on that score to exclaim: "There's only one way of bringing about the League. Leave off talking about the President and hang the Kaiser."

CRUSHED VIOLETS

"Good God! I forgot the violets!" exclaimed Walter Savage Landor, after he had thrown his cook out of the window. This happened at Fiesole, near Florence, and within one year of a century ago. The great prose master had a rather excitable temperament, as Charles Dickens has testified. (The novelist put him in Bleak House as Boythorn — "with the genius and much else left out," as Havelock Ellis says.) Landor dearly loved his flowers, and in his dismay he gave birth to a classic phrase. Nowadays we would gladly put a chef on the throne, so debased has become the world's cuisine. But Landor was an aristocrat masquerading as a fierce democrat and his gesture was a typical one, and in the gentlemanly interest; we might say a gentleman's prerogative, one that has gone quite out of fashion.

I am minded of his despairing cry when I think of Walter Pater. A member of the delicious Hermione's family, indelibly recorded by Don Marquis, asked me once upon a time if the prose of Pater didn't remind me of crushed violets. I related then and there the adventure of Landor's cook and the flowerbed. Her answer threw much light on her mentality: "I wonder what the cook said?" she asked. But Pater prose and crushed violets! For the life of me I can't bridge this gulf of the dissimilar. Some of Whistler is an indigestion of strawberries and cream; but Pater and violets! Walter Pater wasn't as "precious," as insipid, as his imitators.

On a certain occasion Matthew Arnold advised Frederic Harrison to "flee Carlylese as the very devil," and doubtless would have given the same advice regarding Paterese. It is true Pater is dangerous for students. This theme of style, so admirably vivified in Sir Walter Raleigh's monograph — the best we know of; Robert Louis Stevenson's essay on the technical elements of style is too technical, valuable as it is — has been worn threadbare from Aristotle to Renton and his Logic of Style. Pater produced slowly — he wrote five books in twenty years, at the rate of an essay or two every year, thus matching Flaubert in his tormented production. The chief accusation brought against the Pater method of working and his consequent style is its lack of spontaneity; it is not a natural style. But a "natural style," so called, is not encountered in its full flowering more than a half dozen times during the course of a century; perhaps that figure is an exaggeration. The French write all but flawless prose. To match Flaubert, Renan, or Anatole France we must go to Ruskin, Newman, and Pater. When we say, "Let us write simple, straightforward English," we are setting a standard that has been reached only by Thackeray, Newman, Arnold, and how few others? There are as many victims of the "natural English" formula as there are of the "artificial" formula of Pater and Stevenson. The first-named write careless, flabby, colorless, undistinguished, lean commercial English, and pass unnoticed in the vast whirlpool of universal mediocrity, where the cliché is lord of the paragraph. The others, victims to a misguided ideal of affected "fine writing," are more easily detected and denounced by purists, pedants, and other sultry professorial persons. A master, Renan, disliked the teaching of "style" per se — as if the secret could be imparted — yet he toiled over his manuscripts. We recall the Flaubert case. With Pater one should not rush to the conclusion, because he produced slowly, that he was of an artificiality all compact. For him prose was a fine art. He could no more have used a phrase coined by another than he could have worn the other man's hat. He embroidered upon the canvas of his themes the grave and lovely phrases we so envy and admire. Prose — "cette ancienne et très jalouse chose," as it was described by Stéphane Mallarmé — for Pater was at once a pattern and a cadence, a picture and a song. Never suggesting hybrid "poetic-prose," the stillness of his style — atmospheric, languorous, sounding sweet undertones — is always in the true rhythm of prose. Speed is absent. The tempo is usually lenten. Brilliancy is not pursued; there is a hieratic, almost episcopal, pomp. The sentences uncoil their many-colored lengths; there are echoes, repercussions, tonal imagery, and melodic evocation; there is clause within clause that occasionally confuse; for compensation we are given harmonies newly orchestrated, as salient, as mordant, and as subtly rare as chords in the music of Brahms or Debussy. Sane prose it always is; but seldom simple. It is extremely personal, and while it may not make music for every ear, it is exquisitely adapted to the idea it garbs. Read Ruskin aloud and then apply the same vocal test to Pater, and the magnificent harmonies of the older man will conquer your ear by storm; but Pater, like Newman, will make your ear captive in a persuasive snare more delicately varied, and with modulations more enchanting. Never oratorical, in eloquence slightly muffled, the last manner of Pater hinted at newer combinations. Of his prose we may say, quoting his own words concerning another theme: "It is beauty wrought from within, . . . the deposit, little cell by cell, of strange thoughts and fantastic reveries and exquisite passions."

The prose of Jeremy Taylor is more impassioned, Sir Thomas Browne's richer and full of flashing conceits; there are deeper organ tones in De Quincey, and Ruskin excels in effects, rhythmic and sonorous; but the prose of Pater is more sinuous, subtle, more felicitous, and in its essence consummately intense. Morbid it is, sometimes, and its rich polyphony palls if one is not in the mood, and in greater measure than the prose of classic masters, for the world is older and Pater was often weary of life. But suggestions of morbidity may be found in every writer from Plato to Dante, from Dante to Shakespeare and Goethe. It is but the faint spice of mortality which lends a stimulating if sharp perfume to all literatures. Beautiful art is always challenged as corrupting. There may be a grain of truth in the accusation. Man cannot live by wisdom alone, so art was invented by him to console, to disquiet, to arouse. Art may be a dangerous adventure and also an anodyne, like religion. And unhappily we are losing our taste for adventuring amidst dangerous ideas. Once deprived of moral self-determination, of the right of private judgment, man soon relapses into a vegetable existence. Whenever a new poet or philosopher appears he is straightway accused of tampering with the moral currency. This is only mediocrity's mode of adjusting too marked mental disproportions. Difference engenders hatred. In this period, when art and literature are violently despised and persecuted, do not let us be frightened by the word "wicked." For my part, as an old practitioner in literary and artistic poisons, I have never encountered a book or a picture or a sonata that was so immoral as to kill at twenty paces. So let us cheer up, read Pater, Baudelaire, and the Bible — from which they derive — and blench not before the dissonant batteries of the Neo-Scythian composers.

There is another Pater, one far removed from the weaver of colored silken phrases. If he recalls the richness of Keats in the texture of his prose, he can also suggest the aridity of Spencer. There are essays of his as cold, as logically adamant, and as tortuous as sentences in the Synthetic Philosophy. Luckily his tendency to abstract reasoning was subdued by the humanism of his temper. There are not many "purple panels" in his prose; "purple" in the De Quincey or Ruskin manner; no "fringes of the north star" style. He never wrote in sheer display. For the boorish rhetoric and apish attitudes of much modern writing he betrayed no sympathy. His critical range is catholic. Consider his essays on Lamb, Coleridge, Wordsworth, Winckelmann, not to mention those finely wrought masterpieces, the studies of Da Vinci, Giorgione, Botticelli, Joachim du Bellay. Even the newly gathered minor essays, slight as they are in theme and treatment, reveal the master.

Somewhat cloistered in his attitude toward the normal world of work, often the artist for art's sake, he may never trouble the main currents of literature; but he will always be a writer for writers, a critic for critics. Little books may have their destiny. Pater was a thinker whose vision pierces the shell of appearances, the composer of a polyphonic prose-music which echoes a harmonious adagio heard within the spaces of a Gothic cathedral, through the multi-colored windows of which filters alien daylight. It was

a favorite contention of his that all the arts
aspire toward the condition of music.   This idea
is the keynote of Walter Pater, mystic and musician, who, like his own Marius the Epicurean,
carried, his life long, "in his bosom across a
crowded public place — his own soul."   And
yet —— !

BAUDELAIRE'S LETTERS TO HIS
MOTHER

WHEN a well-known man dies in England
they ask: What did he do? In France: How
did he do it? In the United States: How much
did he leave? But the Socialist in every land
says: He didn't do it! The poetic production
of Charles Baudelaire, if put to the same test
questions, might easily be conceived as evoking
even more variety of responses. Baudelaire
has said that nations produce great men against
their will. While his position in the poetic
firmament of France is that of a star of the
first magnitude, there are, nevertheless, dissi-
dents, especially among foreign critics, who
either cannot or will not admit what is become
a truism in French criticism. And the critical
literature concerning the poet grows apace.
His letters to his mother, recently published,
make a volume admirably calculated to illumi-
nate the character of the man. It contains a
preface and notes by Jacques Crépet, who, it
may be remembered, assisted his father, Eu-
gène Crépet, in the biographical study of Baudelaire, a definitive study, one is tempted to add,
for it dissipated a lot of legends (most of them
fabricated by the poet himself) and put his
house of life into some sort of order. Above

all, it cleared up the rather murky atmosphere of his relations with Jeanne Duval, his Black Venus, who was in reality a young woman with hardly a moiety of African blood in her veins. But she served as a peg for the poet upon which to hang some of his most acrid and lovely verse, therefore she must pass muster in any estimate of his disquieting genius.

Withal, the exegetical literature is not large. George Saintsbury introduced him to English readers, although Algernon Charles Swinburne had in practice, if not by precept, brought his "poisonous honey from France" — Tennyson's phrase. The Letters (1841–66) were published in 1907 by the *Mercure de France*, which also fathered a bulky volume devoted to the posthumous works (1908). La Plume had in 1893 republished from the Belgian edition the condemned pieces from Les Fleurs du Mal, with an extraordinary frontispiece by the Belgian etcher, Armand Rassenfosse. There are some poetic numbers in this rare plaque — eagerly sought for by lovers of exotic literature — yet the majority of the pieces must be read book in one hand, the other hand tightly closing the nostrils. These suppressed poems are not the best Baudelairia. Féli Gautier's illustrated pamphlet (Editions de la Plume) is the most succinct account of the poet. There is also a handy little volume by Alphonse Seché and Jules Bertaut, garnered from various sources, yet of critical merit. And in 1917, during the heat of conflict, Guillaume

Apollinaire prefaced the definitive text of the poems and said some pertinent things of Baudelaire. He calls the poet the literary son of Choderlos de Laclos and Edgar Poe — a shuddering combination, indeed.

The previous collection of Letters are of more general interest, for they are addressed to his most distinguished contemporaries — painters, poets, musicians — his friend Richard Wagner among the rest — men of letters and aristocratic ladies. But in the Letters to his mother, Mme. Aupick, the atmosphere is more dramatic, more intense. A duel is fought from his school days to the year previous to his death; the duel of a man, half crazed with alcohol and drugs, and a mother who failed to understand the queer duckling of genius she had hatched out in her first marriage. Demands for money fill the majority of these epistles. Pleas for his poetic work also loom largely, but poverty is the leading motive throughout. We catch more than a profile portrait of the mother; it is not always winning or "motherly." How could it be with such a son? A half-Hamlet, he was jealous of his mother's second husband. It was one of the determining causes in his morbid growth. How has his case so long escaped the psychiatrists of the psychoanalytic school? Albert Mordell, in his Erotic Element in Literature, could have found him a better subject than Stendhal for the Œdipus-complex. Notwithstanding his Flowers of Evil, his diabolic and dandical poses, Baude-

laire was not a wicked-hearted man. Weak he
was rather than depraved. And too curious of
certain matters. He did explore the subcellars
of the soul, dive into cesspools, and expose putrid
sores. A scavenger poet, nevertheless a great
poet, the greatest since Hugo. To-day his suc-
cessor to the purple is Gabriele d'Annunzio.

There was decay in Baudelaire's bones, a
necrosis of the moral nature, yet no more fervent
believer among latter-day poets in God and his
Mother has penned their praises, except Ver-
laine. He did lay too much stress on his admiration for Satan, an admiration well-nigh
Manichean, but he argued rightly when he said
that one can't believe in the Almighty and not
believe in the Adversary. Theologically speaking, this is an inexpugnable position; in reality
the world-experiences of the last five years have
uprooted a belief that Satan is bound and sealed
in some hellish solitude. Roaming about and
seeking whom he may devour, would be the con-
sensus of opinion among pious folk. Baudelaire
believed in the devil because he had a personal
devil. Hence his Litanies to Satan, later imi-
tated by Giosuè Carducci in his Hymn to Satan.
"Salute, O Satana, O ribellione, O forza vindice,
Della ragione!" But in his Litanies the French
poet is more explicit; his refrain is "O Satan,
prends pitié de ma longue misère!" And this
from the poet of De profundis clamavi and the
hymn, in Latin, to Saint Francis (Francisco
meæ Laudes)!

A third person has a share in the new Letters, M. Ancelle, the advocate and guardian of the errant Charles. Alternately cajoling and bullying, the letters addressed him by his charge reveal a curious mentality. The father of Baudelaire bequeathed his son about seventy-five thousand francs, soon dissipated by the incipient dandy on pictures, furniture, jewelry, bibelots, clothes, and light o' loves; yet he seemed to think that his guardian was robbing him, that his mother hated him. In the mists and ecstasies of his wild life he saw nothing clearly — except his shining visions, and being of an obstinate nature, he pinned these visions to paper. The history of art can show few more laborious workmen than Baudelaire; his was the technical heroism of which Henry James speaks. Despite his drugs and drinks, he never ceased working, the work of an intellectual galley-slave. He filed his poems. He wrote criticism — Manet, Monet, Cézanne, and Richard Wagner are specimens of his critical clairvoyancy — read his Salons and his splendid tribute to the genius of Wagner in his Music of the Future. Luck seemed against him. Like Balzac, he was forever in debt. His mother came to the rescue; his friends were worn out helping him across perilous pecuniary quagmires. Then he fled to Belgium, a country he loathed, and celebrated that loathing in distasteful verse, there to be stricken with general paralysis, and later to be brought back to Paris, to die cared for by the mother he believed inimical to him. The mystery is that he didn't succumb earlier in his life to the perpetual assaults on his health.

When his mother married the father of the poet, Joseph Francis Baudelaire — or Beaudelaire — she was twenty-seven, her husband sixty-two. By his first marriage the elder Baudelaire had one son, Claude, who, like his half-brother, Charles, died of paralysis. After the death of the father the widow married within a year the handsome, ambitious Aupick, then Chef de Bataillon, Lieutenant-Colonel, decorated with the Legion of Honor, later General and Ambassador to Madrid, Constantinople, and London. Charles was a frail, nervous youth, but, unlike most children of genius, he was an excellent scholar and won brilliant prizes at college. In this d'Annunzio resembled him. His stepfather was proud of him. From the Royal College at Lyons Charles went to the Lycée Louis-le-Grand, Paris, but was expelled in 1839. (He was born in 1821, also the birth year of Flaubert.) Troubles soon began at home. He disdained his mother and quarrelled with General Aupick. She has confessed that she was partially to blame; in the flush of her second love she had forgotten her boy. He could not forget nor forgive what he called her infidelity to the memory of his father. Hamlet-like, he was inconsolable. The worthy Bishop of Montpelier, an old family friend, said that

Charles was a little crazy; that second marriages usually bring woe in their train. The young poet contented himself with muttering: "When a mother has such a son she doesn't remarry." The reverse was probably the truth. He wrote in his journal: "My ancestors idiots or maniacs . . . all victims of terrible passions"; which was another of his exaggerations. His father was a student, a practical man, a steady-going bourgeois. On the paternal side the grandfather of Charles was a Champenois peasant; his mother's people presumably were of Normandy, though little is known of her forebears. Charles believed himself lost from the time his half-brother was stricken with paralysis, as well he might. Like many others, Baudelaire was a victim to a malady the origins of which were little known in his day. He also believed that his own instability of temperament was the result of the disparity of years in his parents.

In the heyday of his blood he was perverse. Let us credit him with contradicting the Byronic notion that ennui can be best cured by evil ways; sin, Baudelaire found the saddest of diversions. Despite Théophile Gautier's stories about the hashish club, Catulle Mendès denies that the poet was addicted to the hemp habit. What the majority of mankind does not know concerning the habits of literary workers is this prime fact: that men who toil writing poetry — and there is no mental toil comparable to it, not even the higher mathematics — cannot indulge in drink or opium without speedy collapse. The old-fashioned ideas of "inspiration," spontaneity, easy improvisation, of the sudden bolt from heaven, are delusions still hugged by the world. To be told that Chopin filed at his music for years, that in his smithy Beethoven forged his thunderbolts in the sweat of his sooty brows, that Manet slaved like a dock laborer, that Baudelaire was a mechanic in his devotion to work, may be a disillusion for the sentimental. Yet such is the case. Minerva springing full-fledged from Jupiter's skull is a pretty fancy, but Balzac and Flaubert did not encourage that fancy. Work literally killed them, as it killed Poe and Jules de Goncourt. Maupassant went insane because he would work and he would play the same day. Baudelaire worked and worried. His debts haunted him. His constitution was undoubtedly flawed, but that his life was one prolonged debauch is a nightmare of the moral police in some white cotton nightcap country. These letters to his mother are the most human of documents and they prove the contrary. Charles Baudelaire is the saddest and the profoundest poet in modern literature.

Speaking of Nietzsche, I am reminded of the study by William M. Salter, Nietzsche the Thinker, which happened to be published here at an inopportune time (1917). It is the most satisfactory exposition of the ideas of the great poet-philosopher, who, even if he did not create an inclosed system, has given birth to original and suggestive ideas. Mr. Salter has, of course, exploded the erroneous notion that Nietzsche was persona grata with the Prussians. A letter in my possession, though not addressed to me — alas! I have but one written to me — begins thus: "Woe to the victors, for they shall be vanquished!" A veritable prophecy. This was dated 1875, and alluded to the Franco-Prussian War, the consequences of which sorrowed the soul of Nietzsche. The Salter book is testimony to American scholarship; cogent, bold, brilliant, and conclusive.

THE TWO TEMPTATIONS

THE two Temptations! Sounds melodramatic, doesn't it? But it only refers to the various versions of a great book. All good Flaubertians will rejoice to learn that the earlier draft of Flaubert's Temptation of St. Antony, has been given a fitting English garb. This translation is made from the 1849 and 1856 manuscripts, edited by Louis Bertrand, and is by René Francis. The preface is by Sir Gaston Maspero, distinguished archæologist, and there is also a prefatory note by Louis Bertrand. This version must not be confounded with the definitive one of 1874, Englished in superlative fashion by Lafcadio Hearn and published here in 1910. The new and bulky volume, admirably printed and copiously illustrated, is a literary curiosity without which no Flaubert collection would be complete. To be sure, Flaubert translated is Flaubert traduced, for as Arthur Symons has written, Flaubert is difficult to translate because he has no fixed rhythm.

"His prose keeps step with no regular march music. He invents the rhythm of every sentence; he changes his cadence with every mood or for the convenience of every fact. He has no theory of beauty in form apart from what it expresses. For him form is a living thing, the physical body of thought, which it clothes and interprets. Compare the style," continues Mr. Symons, "of Flaubert in his books and you will find that each book has its own rhythm, perfectly appropriate to its subject-matter. In Chateaubriand, Gautier, even Baudelaire, the cadence is always the same; the most exquisite word painting of Gautier can be translated rhythm for rhythm without difficulty into English. Once you have mastered the tune you have merely to go on; every verse will be the same." Not so with Flaubert. His is truly polyphonic prose — a phrase, by the way, that Amy Lowell uses to describe an amorphous form of prose and poetry. When I invented the combination years ago I meant only prose, what George Saintsbury would call "numerous prose." See his valuable critical History of English Prose Rhythm.

While on a visit in 1845, Flaubert visited Genoa. There, in the Palace Balbi-Senarega — not at the Doria, as Maxime du Camp wrote with his accustomed carelessness — the French writer saw an old picture by Breughel (probably Pieter the younger, surnamed Hell-Breughel) that represents a Temptation of St. Antony. It is dingy in color and far from a masterpiece. But Flaubert, who loved the grotesque, procured an engraving of this picture, and it hung till the day of his death in his study at Croisset, near Rouen. I have seen it, as it still hangs in

the Flaubert Museum there. This picture was
the spring-board for his two Temptations.
Their germ may be found in his mystery play,
Smarh, with its demon and its metaphysical
coloring. But Breughel surely set into motion
the mental machinery of the Temptation, which
never stopped whirring till 1874.

The first draft of the Temptation was begun
May 24, 1848, and finished September 12, 1849.
The manuscript numbered five hundred and
forty pages. Set aside for Madame Bovary,
this draft was again taken up and the second
version was made in 1856; when finished the
manuscript was reduced to one hundred and
ninety-three pages. Not satisfied, Flaubert
returned to the work in 1872, and when ready
for publication in 1874 the number of pages
was one hundred and thirty-six; even then he
cut out from ten chapters, three. When a few
years later the 1856 version was given to the
world French critics were astonished to find it
so different from the definitive version of 1874.
The critical taste of Flaubert was vindicated.
His was true technical heroism. Reading in
1849 the earliest version to his friends Bouilhet
and Du Camp he had been bidden to burn the
stuff; instead he boiled it down into the 1856
version. To his dearest friend, Ivan Turgénieff,
he submitted his 1872 draft. Thus it came that
the wonderfully colored psychic and philosophic
panorama, this Gulliver-like excursion round
and about the master-ideas and religions of the

antique and early Christian worlds was at last published.

All the youthful Flaubert, the "spouter" of blazing phrases, the lover of jewelled words, of picturesque and monstrous ideas and situations is in the first turbulent version of the Temptation; in the definitive version he is more critical, historical. As his emotions cooled with the years, Flaubert had grown intellectually. The first Temptation is romantic, religious; the 1874 is better composed and sceptical. Arranged more dramatically than the first, the author's leanings toward Oriental mysticism and the dominating ideas of the classic world are better revealed in the last version. The psychological gradations of character are more clearly indicated in this version. We cannot agree with Louis Bertrand, editor of the 1856 version, that it is superior to the version of 1874. It seems more novel, that's all. Flaubert was never so much the surgeon as when he operated upon this manuscript. He often hesitated, he always suffered, but he never flinched when his mind was fully resolved. It is for the student a subject of enthralling interest to follow the slow growth of these various versions.

"Since Goethe," would be a suggestive title for an essay on the various epics written since his death. The list would not be large. In France there are only the barren rhetorical exercises of Edgar Quinet's Ahasuerus, the insurrectionary poems of Hugo and the frigidly faultless verse of Leconte de Lisle. But a work of such profound depth and heroic power as Faust there is not, except the Temptation of St. Antony, which is impregnated by the Faustian spirit — though in its development poles apart from the older poem — that we are not surprised when we learn that the youthful Flaubert was a passionate admirer of Goethe, even addressing to his memory a long poem in alexandrines. The Temptation is the only poem — despite its prose it is poetic — that may be classed with Brand or Zarathushtra. At times, in its sweep of execution and grandeur of conception, it grazes certain episodes in Faust.

But though it may excel in verbal beauty or in its imaginative presentation of the problems of volition, it falls short of Goethe's ethical vision. Faust is a man who wills. "In the beginning was the act." Antony is static, not dynamic. Faust is tempted by Mephisto, yet does not lose his soul. Flaubert's hermit resists Satan at his subtlest; withal, we do not feel that his soul is as much worth the saving as Faust's. Man for man, Faust is the more significant; Antony is narrow-minded; indeed, almost besotted by superstition. He crystallizes, also symbolizes, a vanished period of mythology. Faust stands for the man of the present, and in the second part of the poem the man of the future. Ideas are the heroes of Flaubert's epic, though St. Antony's is a metaphysical history, not a human one like Faust's.

But to Faust alone may the Temptation be compared. George Saintsbury has pronounced this masterpiece to be the most perfect example extant of dream literature. And precisely because of its precision in details, its astounding architectonic and its rich-hued waking hallucinations.

THE FLAUBERT ANNIVERSARY

IT is a holy and a wholesome act to visit the grave of a genius, for the memories there aroused may serve as a consolation and an inspiration in our spiritually arid existence. I often thought of this at Rouen when I went there to visit the tomb of Gustave Flaubert, so happily described by François Coppée as The Beethoven of French Prose. A quarter of a century ago I protested in newspapers and books against the tardy official recognition accorded one of the great prose masters of France — which means the world — and one of the most marvellous among novelists. In the Solferino Gardens at Rouen there is the marble memorial by the sculptor Chapu, and on the heights of the Monumental Cemetery, in the Flaubert family plot — Flaubert's father was a distinguished surgeon — and not far from the Joan of Arc monument, lie the remains of the author of Madame Bovary. His celebrated pupil, Guy de Maupassant, is also remembered in the Solferino Gardens by a statue; another may be seen in the Parc Monceau. But at the time I began urging some form of a memorial to the master of masters nothing had been done. Since then the government has made of the old Flaubert home at Croisset, a half-hour from Rouen, down the

Seine, a worthy memorial. The house in which such masterpieces as Madame Bovary, Salammbô, Sentimental Education, The Temptation of St. Antony, Bouvard and Pécuchet, and the Three Tales were created is now a Flaubert museum. Abbé Prevost is said to have written Manon Lescaut there. The old house still stands, though decaying. Flaubert's study is, however, in fair preservation. The paternal home, occupying a part of the little park, was a dismantled manufactory when last I saw the place.

The faithful Colange, for twenty years servitor in the Flaubert household, kept a café in the neighborhood, and was always ready to talk of his master, of Mme. Flaubert, the mother. In vain I tried to get a photograph of that lady. Colange would not sell it, would not even have it reproduced. I have seen the picture of Dr. Achille Flaubert, but I am more interested in the mothers of men of genius, and I can recall no edition of the works containing the portrait of Mme. Flaubert. But I recall her features. A sweet, mild, intelligent face, betraying evidences of sorrow and resignation. The typical mother. Her son was a celibate, and, with the exception of Louise Colet, he never gave his mother any worriment over women. And it was that lady, whose portrait was recently exhibited at the Courbet retrospective exhibition in the Metropolitan Museum, who was the disturber, not Flaubert. There had been an affair, and understanding the honorable nature of the man, the wily humbug Louise endeavored to make trouble. She wrote Mme. Flaubert, a deeply pious woman; she harried Gustave, who, like most literary psychologists and sounders of feminine souls, was naïve in the practical conduct of his love-affairs. The epitaph of Louise Colet was composed by Maxime Ducamp: "Here lies the woman who compromised Victor Cousin, made Alfred de Musset ridiculous, and tried to assassinate Alphonse Karr; requiescat in pace." A mean, spiteful masculine witticism this, though well deserved. Of Ducamp a like epitaph might be fabricated: Hic jacet the man who slandered Baudelaire, traduced his loving friend Gustave Flaubert, and who was critically snuffed out of existence by Guy de Maupassant.

I have preserved a card sent to me by Mme. Franklin Grout, dated from Villa Tanit, Antibes, in which she expressed her gratitude for several things I wrote regarding the necessity of a Flaubert museum at Croisset; also for the truth in the Ducamp matter. Mme. Grout was the Caroline Commanville of the Flaubert correspondence, the beloved niece of the master, for whom he sacrificed his personal fortune, a considerable one for a man of letters forty years ago (about one million two hundred thousand francs). Her husband, M. Commanville, had suffered from reverses, and Flaubert, the supposed egoist, cold-blooded, self-centred, an epicurean of literature, calmly deprived himself of his last franc and, nearly sixty years of age, went into harness. His noble act was accomplished without the flaring of trumpets. There were no publishers' "blurbs" then; nowadays this transaction in hearts and bonds would be yawped to the thousand winds of publicity; luckily, the sensitive great man was spared that vulgar fate. After the death of her husband, Caroline Commanville remarried; her second husband was the Dr. Grout who attended Guy de Maupassant during his fatal illness at the famous Maison Blanche.

Think of it! I saw the great Flaubert in the flesh. I may quote Browning: "Ah, did you once see Shelley plain, and did he stop and speak to you?" . . . Set me down as hopelessly romantic, as a cultivator of the cult of great artists in an age when there are only imitators or pigmies. It's born in me, this species of artistic snobbery. I can't help it. Every now and then some professorial rabbit pokes its pink snout from the academic hutch and passionately pipes, "Romance is the ruin of the world!" and retires on gliding paws. After his naughty proclamation I always take down from the shelf Alice in Wonderland and read with renewed delight the conversation of the Mad Hatter and the March Hare. No romance in the world? Of that particular professorial rabbit Daisy Ashford might say: Render unto

Cæsar's wife the things that are suspicious!
Even academic rabbits are romantic; else their
breeding propensities have been enormously
exaggerated. Flaubert is my romance.

Above all, Flaubert was a musician, a musical
poet. His ear was the final court of appeal,
and to make sonorous cadences in a language
that lacks the essential richness, the diapasonic
undertow of the English, is just short of the
miraculous. Until the time of Chateaubriand
and Victor Hugo the French language was less
a liquid, plastic collocation of sounds than a
formal pattern, despite the clarity and precision
of the eighteenth century; one must go back to
the sixteenth and seventeenth centuries for
richer, more pregnant speech. Omnipresent
with Flaubert was the musician's idea of composing a masterpiece that should float because
of its sheer style. Lyric verbal ecstasy quite
overpowered him. He was born December 21,
1821. As Henry James has said, he is one of
the glories of French literature. Doubtless
there will be a fitting commemoration of his
one hundredth birth anniversary two years
hence, and I hope that America will be represented at Rouen on that occasion.

ROOSEVELT AND BRANDES

My first meeting with Theodore Roosevelt, though brief, will be ever memorable for me. I was not precisely "summoned" to Oyster Bay on Election Day early in November, 1915, though I gladly accepted Col. Roosevelt's invitation in the light of a "royal command," and went over to Long Island in company with John Quinn, who had arranged the meeting, and Francis J. Heney, once public prosecutor in San Francisco. I had received several letters from the Colonel of Colonels, of which I recall two significant sentences. One ended: "What a trump John Quinn is!" The other begins: "I have just received your New Cosmopolis. My son Kermit, whose special delight is New York, would probably appreciate it more than I do, for I am a countryman rather than a man of the pavements." Now, I had always thought of Theodore Roosevelt as a "man of the pavements," notwithstanding his delight in rough-riding across Western prairies. Personally I found him the reverse of either: a scholarly man, fond of music and the fine arts — he showed me a number of canvases by the late Marcius Simmons, a young American painter, who had been greatly influenced by Turner. The colonel had an excellent library of Colonial literature, and was fond of digging out pregnant sentences for quotation in his speeches from early preachers and statesmen. He appeared to be interested in my comparison between his prose style and the prose style of President Woodrow Wilson: the one swift, concise, full of affirmations, striking sentences, and notable for its absence of glitter. For the colonel reality was greater than rhetoric; while the prose of Mr. Wilson is eminently professorial, preserving as it does a nice balance of sound and sense; above all, "literary" prose, the prose of the study, never dynamic, seldom brilliant; prose "standardized," eighteenth-century, smooth, sinuous, flexible, and ever-illuding prose.

My distinguished host showed some of the trophies he had acquired in Europe when on that historic grand tour; and, as I had not visited him in the guise of a professional interviewer, I did not write at the time of what I saw; but now I may do so without violating the intimacies of private hospitality. One thing that interested me was a photograph of the late Andrew Carnegie, taken in Berlin during the military manœuvres; both Carnegie and Roosevelt had been guests of William Hohenzollern, then Kaiser. I told the colonel that I had been present at the formal opening of the Peace Palace, in September, 1913, at The Hague, and that the day had been so hot that all Holland, there represented, had fled to the beach at Scheveningen, adding that I believed the palace eventually would be turned into the handsomest café in Europe; and I had printed this prophecy (?) in *The Times Sunday Magazine*, when reporting the solemn humbuggery of the peaceful house-warming.

War was discussed with all the zest of the wonderful man. One question I permitted myself: "Colonel, would the Lusitania have been sunk if you had been in the White House?" Snapping his formidable jaw, he exclaimed: "There would have been no Lusitania incident if I had been President."

Among other various topics the colonel descanted on the poetical merits of George Cabot Lodge, son of Senator Henry Cabot Lodge, who died in the very harvest time of his genius. In his introduction to the two volumes of Poems and Dramas, Theodore Roosevelt has never written with such a happy mingling of perspicacity and tempered enthusiasm. Among the younger American poets I find Lodge of importance, not along because of his potential promise, but because of his actual performance. An authentic poet, his versatility is marked. In his sonnets and lyrics he paid the admiring tribute of youth to Milton, Wordsworth, Tennyson, Browning, Meredith, and Swinburne. He could mimic Walt Whitman, who is fatally easy to parody, and he early succumbed to Schopenhauer and Baudelaire. In at least one of his dramas I found the cosmic ecstasy of Nietzsche; also the doctrine of the Eternal Return. But young Lodge had assimilated a half dozen cultures, and passed far out to sea the perilous rocks of imitation, upon which so many lesser talents have come to grief. When as an achievement we consider his Herakles we are amazed at its maturity of thought and technical finish. The poet, the Maker, confronts us, and in reclothing the antique and tragic myth with his own lovely language he is, nevertheless, a "modern." I know few poets of the new school who may boast this sense of the vital present, added to a divination and an evocation of "old, unhappy far-off things and battles long ago." His figures are not fashioned by academic black magic, but are vital beings, loving, trusting, suffering, and in conflict with ineluctable destiny. He had the lyric art, also the architectural. He was a singer and a builder of the lofty rhyme. His handling of complex forms and abstruse rhymes was remarkable. George Cabot Lodge possessed both voice and vision. His life, by Henry Adams, shows him to have been a young man beloved by his friends, among whom were Jonathan Stickney Trumbull, Langdon Mitchell, and the late Sir Cecil Spring-Rice. When I met him in Paris he was a student at the Sorbonne. It was about 1896. A charming youth. I may only add now my humble mite of admiration to the manes of this dead genius.

When I saw Dr. Georg Brandes at the Hotel Astor a few months before the outbreak of the Great War I told him that he resembled the bust

made of him by Klinger. It was the first time
I had talked to the celebrated Danish author, to
whom I had dedicated Egoists. Then past
seventy, as active as a young man, I could see
no reason why he shouldn't live to be a centenarian. An active brain is lodged in his nimble
body. I had made up my mind to ask him no
questions about America. I found him in a
rage over the way he was misquoted by some of
the interviewers. It should be remembered that
primarily he is a cosmopolitan thinker. He
writes in English, French, German, and Danish
with equal ease. As to the provinciality of our
country's literature and the seven arts he has
definite opinions; but he was polite enough not
to rub them in on me. He was accused of finding his favorite reading in the "works" of Jack
London! That idea amused him. Among our
"moderns" it is Frank Norris he likes; a slight
difference, indeed. Emerson, Poe, Whitman interested him, though not as iconoclasts or path-
finders. The originality of this trinity he didn't
dwell upon; made-over Europeans, he called
them; Emerson and German transcendental
philosophy; Poe and E. T. W. Hoffmann; Whitman and Ossian — Walt's rugged speech is a
windy parody of MacPherson's, and Ossian himself is a windy parody of the Old Testament
style.

Brandes is an iconoclast, a radical, a non-
conformist born, and more often a No-Sayer
than a Yes-Sayer. The many-headed monster

has no message for him. As he was the first
European critic to give us true pictures of Ibsen
and Nietzsche, I led him to speak of the poet-
philosopher. At Baireuth, where I had gone to
hear the Wagner music-drama at its fountain-
head — and very muddy was the music-making,
I am sorry to say — I was shown the house
where was born Max Stirner. My friend said:
"When the very name of Richard Wagner is
forgotten, Stirner's will be in the mouth of the
world." Of course, this sounded improbable.
I know Stirner's book, The Ego and Its Own,
knew his real name, Johann Kaspar Schmidt,
and that he had been a poor, half-starved school-
master in Berlin, and, in 1845, imprisoned by the
Prussian Government. This intellectual anarch
— rather call him nihilist, for, compared with
his nihilism, Bakunin's is only revolutionary re-
sistance — was to become later the most powerful disrupting force in Europe! I couldn't believe it. But now I recall my friend's prophecy
when I read of the doings of the Russian Bol-
sheviki. Not Nietzsche, but Stirner, has been
the real motor force in the contemporary revolution. No half-way house of socialism for the
Reds! And that is the lesson of Artzibachev's
Sanine, the import of which the majority of
critics missed, partially because of the imperfect
English translation — many suppressions — and
also because they missed the significance of the
new man, who, while continuing the realistic
tradition of Dostoievsky and Tolstoy, was di-

ametrically opposed to their sentimental Brother-
hood of Man — toujours that old fallacy of
Rousseau! — and preached the fiercest individualism, violently repudiating Nietzsche and his
aristocratic individualism. It may be said in
passing that a reaction to individualism is bound
to come; the lesson of the war will not be lost.
Nor the teaching of Emerson. After the present
overt suppression of the individual, the pendulum will surely swing from tyrannical socialism to the greater freedom of the individual.
And it can't come quickly enough here in
America.

Dr. Brandes sets more store by Nietzsche
than Stirner; he was the first to call Nietzsche
a "radical aristocrat." We switched to the
theme of Strindberg. Brandes said: "Yes, he
was mad. Once he visited me and told me of a
call he had made at a lunatic asylum near
Stockholm. He rang the bell and asked the
physician if he — Strindberg, the greatest of
dramatists — was crazy; to which the doctor
replied: 'My dear Mr. Strindberg, if you will
only consent to stay with me six weeks and talk
with me every day, I promise to answer your
question.'" After that Brandes had no doubts
on the question. Brandes is not only the dis-
coverer of Ibsen, Nietzsche, and Strindberg, but
he himself is a revaluer of old valuations.
Therein lies his significance for this generation.
In 1888 he wrote to Nietzsche: "I have been the
best hated man in the north for the last four

years. The newspapers rave against me every
day, especially since my long feud with Bjornson,
in which all the 'moral' German newspapers
take sides against me." . . . To-day he is regarded as a reactionary by the Reds. The affections of Brandes have always been bestowed
upon the literatures of England and France.
Of his Main Currents, Maurice Bigeon has said
that Brandes did for the nineteenth century
what Sainte-Beuve did for the seventeenth century in his History of Port Royal. What is vital,
what makes for progress, what has lasting influence in social life? asks the Dane in his Main
Currents. He will remain the archetype of
cosmopolitan critics for future generations. A
humanist, the mind of Brandes is steel-colored.
Ductile, when white-hot, it flows like lava from
a volcano in eruption; but always is it steel,
whether liquefied or rigid. Pre-eminently it is
the fighting mind. He objects to being described as "brilliant." The model of Brandes
as a portrait-painter of ideas and individuals is
Velasquez, because "Velasquez is not brilliant,
but true."

Yet he is brilliant and lucid, and steel-like,
whether writing of Shakespeare or Lassalle.
An ardent upholder of Taine and the psychology
of race, he contends that in the individual, not
in the people, lies the only hope for progress.
He is altogether for the psychology of the individual. Like Carlyle, he has the cult of the
great man. The fundamental question is —

can the well-being of the race, which is the end of all effort, be attained without great men? "I say no, and again, no!" he cries. He is a firm believer in the axiom that every tub should stand on its own bottom; and in our earthly pasture, where the sheep think, act, or vote to order, the lesson of Brandes is "writ clear": To myself be true! that truth set forth with double facets by Ibsen in Peer Gynt and Brand. Also by Emerson. Beware of the Bogy — the cowardly spirit of compromise, with its sneaking prudent advice; Go around! For mobs and mob-made laws Georg Brandes has a mighty hatred. He, too, is a radical aristocrat whose motto might be: Blessed are the proud of spirit, for they shall inherit the Kingdom of Earth! With his Hebraic irony he stung to the quick the spiritual sloth of Denmark. His life was made unpleasant at the Copenhagen University; but he had behind him the younger generation. He knew that to write for the intrenched and prejudiced class would be a waste of ink. He exploded his verbal bombs beneath the national ark and blew sky-high stale and false ideals. He became a national figure after he had been recognized as a world critic. Not the polished writer that was Sainte-Beuve, not the possessor of a synthetic intellect like Hippolyte Taine's, Brandes is the broadest-minded man of the three, and upon his shoulders their critical mantles have fallen. Agitated as he was by the war — his letters to me were full of references to it —

he was philosopher enough to plunge into the profoundest work. He has finished two studies on such divergent themes as Goethe and Voltaire. Let us hope both books be given an English garb and speedy publication.

PENNELL TALKS ABOUT ETCHING

WHEN an etcher of Joseph Pennell's caliber talks about his art it behooves both critic and public to sit up and listen. Mr. Pennell is endowed with a special gift for making people sit up. He loves to startle. He is occasionally choleric, he indulges in righteous indignation over the blindness of critics and fumes betimes because of the indifference of the world at large concerning the finer shades of art. Nevertheless, he always says something pertinent, even when it runs contrary to popular opinion, or sneers at critical canons. He is well within his rights as an artist to attack professional critics, for critics and their criticism are a perpetual nuisance — an incontrovertible statement that will, we are sure, be smilingly indorsed by the majority of the pesky critters. In his newly published and magnificently illustrated Etchers and Etching, Mr. Pennell has rendered a genuine service to students and amateurs, for not only does he reveal the secrets of his prison house, but he also reveals with a frankness that is fascinating his opinions of other etchers as compared with his god, Whistler, and incidentally tells his readers that if they do not agree with him they are unvarnished damphools!

Bully old Joe! He is the joy of honest reviewers and the terror of them that are not firmly grounded in their artistic technique. Herein he puts himself through all his familiar paces. Of all the graphic arts, etching is the most superior! Of all etchers, living or dead, James McNeill Whistler is the greatest! From this supreme judgment there is no appeal. And the curious part is that Mr. Pennell gives you chapter and verse to back up his argument. In all that pertained to the delicate and difficult art of etching, Whistler was the master. Not Rembrandt, who was careless as to the printing of his plates, careless as to finesse, and not given to slicking up his work; not Méryon, who was, according to Pennell, an indifferent etcher, and no artist—should be mentioned in company with the peerless Whistler. There is but one Allah in etching, and Pennell is his prophet. Salaam alaiekum! Rembrandt and Whistler? The Apocalypse and the Butterfly!

There is no denying the enthusiasm of an expert. And there is no denial of the proposition that a little knowledge is a dangerous thing in etching as in criticism. Yet there is something to be said for the much-abused critics. Artists who discuss their art are sometimes biassed, to put it mildly. The principal critical pronouncements that have endured were not made by professionals; on the contrary, such writers as Wincklemann, Goethe, Diderot, Blanc, Gautier, Baudelaire — especially Baudelaire — Zola (rather negligible), Goncourt, Roger Marx, Geoffroy, Huysmans, Mauclair, Charles Morice, Octave Mirbeau, R. A. M. Stevenson, George Moore, D. S. MacColl, Lionel Cust, Colvin, Ricci, Sturge Moore, Bernhard Berenson, John Van Dyke, W. C. Brownell, Royal Cortissoz, and others, have contributed more to the right understanding of the plastic arts than any opposing list of painters, sculptors and engravers you may assemble. Sift names and opinions, and for one Fromentin, one Whistler, one Reynolds, you will find a hundred writers who, non-professional as they were and are, have considerably added to our enlightenment in matters artistic.

Not all critics are "men who have failed in literature and art," as Balzac said. The techniques of the various arts are, naturally enough, best known to the practitioners thereof. Yet Curator Frank Weitenkampf of our Public Library has written one of the most valuable books in the arts graphic, How to Appreciate Prints. Its union of technical insight and catholicity of judgment has been justly praised by all discerning etchers. The Discourses of Sir Joshua are, take them by and large, the best of their kind because most temperate. What wouldn't we give for the critical writings of Leonardo da Vinci, whose prose, what we have of it, proves him a master. Vasari is an immortal gossip. William Blake was narrow in his outlook. Fancy ruling out from court the pictures of Rubens! Degas was a wit who abominated art

69

critics more than Mr. Pennell. He abused Huysmans, the first to make public his rare genius. Millet, Rousseau, Constable said interesting things of their art, of their contemporaries. "There is no isolated truth," declared Millet. "A good thing is never done twice," wrote Constable; or Alfred Stevens's definition of art as "nature seen through the prism of an emotion," which epigram evidently Zola remembered in his Experimental Novel. Rodin has also uttered much wisdom. Fromentin's studies of Dutch masters is a standard book, although he missed Vermeer — probably because the work of that master of masters was attributed to other men, notably to Terburg.

Ruskin did much to muddle public opinion with his intemperate praise of Turner and his purblind estimate of Whistler. Who shall deny that he was a force making for good? Walter Pater painted with words, not only making beautiful phrases but memorable criticism. Philip Gilbert Hamerton often blundered, and Pennell impales him, also abundantly quotes from him. The written and reported words of artists are alike precious to layman and critic. That the artist, Mr. Pennell for example, prefers etching to writing is natural; so might the critic if he had the pictorial gift. Art is art, not nature; and criticism is criticism, not always art. It professes to interpret the artist's work, and at best it mirrors his art unavoidably intermingled with the personal temperament of the critic. At the worst, the critic lacks temperament, and when this is the case Heaven help artist and public! Walter Raleigh sums up the question in a sentence: "Criticism, after all, is not to legislate nor to classify, but to raise the dead." The magical art of evocation! Few critics possess the gift, but, then, fewer are the artists who boast it.

That painters — or etchers — can get along without professional criticism we know from history, but that they themselves play the critic successfully is open to doubt. And are they any fairer to younger talent than official criticism? It is an inquiry that should be fraught with significance for professionals. Artists, great and various, have sent forth their pupils into the world. As befits honest criticism, have they at all recognized the pupils of other men; played fair with those whose practice and theory were at the opposite pole to their own? The answer is a decided negative; the examples that might be adduced, legion. Recall what Velasquez said to Salvator Rosa, according to Carl Justi. Salvator had asked the incomparable Spaniard whether he did not think Raphael the best of all the painters he had seen in Italy. Velasquez answered: "To be plain with you, Raphael does not please me at all." In art criticism a Robert Schumann is yet to appear; and notwithstanding his catholicity in taste, Schumann missed Wagner, as did Berlioz. Perhaps Stendhal saw the weakness in such criticisms when he remarked: "Difference engenders hatred."

To leave historical generalities for the particulars of contemporary criticism, let us open a book that has recently appeared, entitled De David à Degas, by Jacques-Emile Blanche, famous portraitist, charming causeur, brilliant penman, sympathetic and sometimes caustic critic. M. Blanche, a painter by "the grace of God," for his talents are many, considers such diverse artists as Ingres, Manet, Renoir, Cézanne, Fantin-Latour — a notably fine estimate — Degas — one of the best essays — Aubrey Beardsley — a masterly miniature of a marvellous draftsman — and the redoubtable Whistler. On page 35 M. Blanche writes of the etchings and lithographs of the American artists, that they were not worthy of their reputation; that the Paris series frankly lean on Méryon, recall his work; others are freer, occasionally pretty, though weak, without character in their picturesque quality of vignette, a genre wherein later Mariano Fortuny excelled! We are here far from Pennell's dictum that Whistler is the greatest etcher that ever lived. What does Jacques Blanche know about etching? probably will be his comment if he reads the critique in question.

And we should quite agree with the etcher if he should make some remark; such one-sided verdict, despite the fact that M. Blanche is to be listened to with respect when he talks of art and artists deserves rebuke! It again confirms the attitude attributed to George Saintsbury that all discussion of contemporaries is conversation, not criticism. Mr. Pennell, who also slaughters the reputations of the living and dead, might put this witticism in his pipe and smoke up. The late William M. Laffan, a practical etcher, one who etched for his bread and butter, as he assured us, wrote in the *Sun* newspaper, of which he was the proprietor at the time of Whistler's death, that the plates of the etcher Whistler would outlive Whistler the painter. Mr. Laffan, who possessed a *flair* for criticism, prophesied aright. He said too that there were no such things as replicas, which is the truth. Many Whistler canvases are sadly deteriorating, critical enthusiasm concerning them is cooling — the artist Whistler is now seen not to be an isolated apparition but a synthesis of his own enthralling self, based on the art of Courbet, Fantin, Albert Moore, the Japanese and the inevitable Velasquez; but the etchings and lithographs of this truly versatile genius, being things of beauty, will be a joy forever. They are his legacy to the elect. And yet, must the "grand manner" of line-engravings irretrievably vanish to make place for the sketchy, fussy etching?

Not only is Brother Pennell — a brother to dragons! — narrow in his estimates of all the great etchers, but he is unjust to workers in other black-and-white mediums. Old-fashioned line-engraving is mechanical, and was so tedious to execute that the process was abandoned for still more mechanical though simpler methods. Not, however, till the patient engravers had bequeathed to art a gallery of stately portraits and landscapes, minutely, if somewhat elaborately, recorded. Etching, be it never so fine, so personal, cannot compete with the masters of line, because etching lacks depth and substance. It is improvisation at the best; at its worst it is almost feline in its scratchings. Mezzotint, too, is a noble art. It is often smudgy, to be sure, but it has tonal splendor, which etching has not, despite the magical suggestion of tone in the Whistler plates. After reading Mr. Pennell's exposition of the pains and perils consequent upon the production of a perfect etching, the finished plates of Marc Antonio, Richard Earlom or Masson's gray-haired man, do not seem a whit more mechanical. There are tricks in all trades. Whistler's supremacy did not alone consist in his virtuosity with the needle, but in his personality as poet and mystic. Rembrandt was greater artist than etcher; in his days the manipulation of material was not so consummate as during the Whistlerian epoch, yet he is by all odds the bigger man. A rude scratch of his and you see the glories of heaven, the gloom of hell. There is a fulness, a richness, a solidity, an architectural quality in Méryon missing in Whistler, Pennell to the contrary notwithstanding. In the evocation of the intangible, the evanescent, of the exquisite, Whistler has never had a rival, and as a technician he is foremost; but George Moore was not far astray when he said that if "Jemmy" had been fifty pounds

74

heavier he might have painted like Velasquez. In the last analysis his work lacks weight, substance, virile power, though not imagination, and that quintessential quality is worth a wilderness of beefy, brilliant, magisterial canvases.

All this is beside the mark, which is the superb Pennell volume. Agree with him or not, he writes with vigor, demolishing shams and humbuggery, and his words, if often intemperate, are prompted by burning sincerity. He is never smug nor self-satisfied. He sees through the hole in our national millstone of art. His ideal is the linear, and at a time when sloppy drawing, barbarous color and grotesque composition have become our shibboleth, his warnings are salutary. His is the cult of beauty for beauty's sake, the only culture in art. Etching to him is the still small voice of an art abused by amateurs, too often tortured by artists (you think of the big plates of Frank Brangwyn). He is fair to the Bohemian, Wenzel Hollar, who, to be seen at his best, one must go to Prague, to the Hollareum, there in the Rudolphinum, where his amazing work may be studied in its entirety.

Mr. Pennell pays a rather grudging tribute to Seymour Haden, while admitting the beauty of his plate, Sunset in Ireland, and he warmed the cockles of our heart by his discriminating praise of the splendid etcher that was Félicien Rops. At the conclusion he peremptorily exclaims: "I know of no other great etchers." Oh, yes, you do, Joseph Pennell! You are too modest by half. Demme, sir, as old Joseph Bagstock would say, old Joey B., begad, sir, you know a chap named Pennell who sometimes etches like an angel. And also lithographs. We'll eat our hat if his scraped mezzotint, Wrens' City, isn't a beautiful plate!

IN PRAISE OF PRINTS

(TO JOSEPH PENNELL)

THE gallery is rather narrow, but long and lofty; the light is diffused and gentle. A tiny staircase leads to mysterious retreats where, Piranesi-like, may be descried other galleries, though not peopled by the prisoners of the fantastic Italian etcher. A familiar voice welcomes the visitor who, weary of the monotonous mobs on the avenue, finds here a haven where, surrounded by the ingratiating arts of black-and-white — mezzotinting, etching, lithograph and line-engraving — he may soothe his soul and rest his bones. The color-scheme is harmonious. A dark panelling, and for the smaller galleries a more cheerful though neutral tone, is observed. Moving slowly about he sees some black spots on the wall; at close range they resolve themselves into ingenious patterns. Stacked in portfolios are prints. On large tables more of them sprawl. In the rear room there is, perhaps, an exhibition of etchings or mezzotints, but seldom of line-engravings. A young Scotsman shows his mettle — the Scotch take to the needle as ducks do to grass. Why are line-engravings never hung nowadays? You are told that taste has changed since the golden age of engraving ruled our walls. And changed for the worse, thinks the fanatic of pure line.

Yonder, above a huge bin, in which are stored rare prints, hangs the Moses of Philippe de Champaigne, engraved by Edelinck. It is a largely moulded composition. The Hebrew law-giver, on whose noble features linger the reflections of Jehovah's divine illumination, the horns of light emanating from Mount Sinai, holds the rod in one hand, supporting with the other the table of the laws. A picture in the grand manner. Therefore, to be passed by in favor of some cryptic scratches on a small plate, a signed proof by an artistic nobody, who designs and etches in a mediocre fashion. Yet his work is eagerly snapped up, while the rhythmic line of Edelinck is not even looked at, rich as it is as an interpretation or artistic performance. "Engraving is so mechanical, don't you think so!" is the usual reason advanced for the neglect of this branch of black-and-white. But, by the same token, no more mechanical than the myriads of fussy little plates of the etchers, for the most part without distinction in style or technique. Nevertheless, etching is a swifter method for registering illusion, and in all the arts — George Moore says there are nine, not seven — the chief thing is to create illusion.

Etching rules. Why? Because an artist of overwhelming genius set upon the art his seal. Because it is a consummate medium for expressing personality, and in all the arts personality is the slogan of the hour. We must bare our souls in our work, cry young folk; the rest, art included, can go hang! But the question is whether these same souls are worth the bother of such exposure. When Rembrandt or Méryon, Whistler, or Pennell exhibited their personalities on their plates the result was: primo, art; secundo, personalities. In a word, not even the perky, cantankerous side of Whistler intervened between his art and his public; the nobler phases of his character, and there were many, shone clear and truthfully. The massive bulk of Rembrandt's personality is reflected in his work with the needle; yet what magnificent art is his! Also a dangerous beacon in a stormy sea for lesser etchers. We love etching. It is the most concise and delicate of all artistic stenography. The scratched line, its symbol, is less complex than the convention of the so-called "steel" engraver, who works in a denser, richer medium, despite the allegation that his is a chilly art. So is sculpture chilly. All depends on the man handling the chisel, or in engraving the wielder of the burin. The richest of the mediums is copper mezzotinted, or scraped plate. It sometimes gives muddy results. Etching has more personal charm; line-engraving is chaster, loftier in style, because more objective.

If a certain formal rigidity or hardness may be urged against the less personal art of line-engraving, what cannot be said of the thin, facile, shallow impressionism of the etched plate? Above all else, structure is lacking, and it is too often a vehicle for piffling anecdote, or the stamping-ground of the superficial dauber. Mezzotint is not always a satisfactory means of expression. It too is mainly reproductive, while its seductive, velvety surfaces may easily degenerate into monotonous formulas. Between Valentine Green and his interpretations of Sir Joshua Reynolds, or Richard Earlom's evocation of an incandescent forge, and the apocalyptic visions of a John Martin, there is the wide and ineluctable gulf of technical mastery. Martin may have been half-mad, like William Blake — as are most mystics viewed in the cold light of worldly reason — but he possessed vision; while Green and Earlom, accomplished copper-scrapers as they were, only saw the superficies of things eternal. To-day John Martin's crude prints may be had for a penny, and the fantastic Piranesi is a drug in the shops. Neither this mezzotinter nor etcher reveals that mysterious "quality" essential in the arts.

It is quality, then, that appeals in etching and mezzotint. It was quality that appealed when the specimen plates of the master engravers were in vogue. Well and good. But why doesn't that quality continue to make the same appeal now to our fastidious taste as it did a half century ago? Naturally enough, the answer is Fashion, which has decreed that the grand old line-engravings be hung in crepuscular hallways. To be sure, there is a corri-

dor in the Pitti Palace, Florence, a sun-flooded
hallway upon which sing the marvels of lyric
line-engravings. Fashion says: admire the
signed etching, coddle the impertinent remarque
proof; Fashion has set topnotch figures for the
English mezzotinters of English portraiture.
By leaps and bounds the prices of Green and
a few of his contemporaries have been mount-
ing, so that to own a Gainsborough or a Sir
Joshua portrait in mezzotint is to proclaim
yourself a person of means. Nor should there
be a protest against these exalted prices. Rare
art can never be high enough; besides, the
domain of mezzotinting will soon be as bare
of practitioners as that of line-engraving. S.
Arlent Edwards is a name that occurs to us
in mezzotinting. Joseph Pennell's essays in
that medium reveal his mastery; while the
artist that is Timothy Cole, stands solitary
as probably the last of distinguished wood-
engravers, as Mandel may be said to have been
the last of famous European line-engravers.

The once haughty elder sister of the arts
graphic is now become their Cinderella. Who
but an anonymous minority cares for the stately
engraved pictures of the past? How their dig-
nified style reproaches the heedless haste of
latter-day photographic reproductions! Yet,
what modern mechanical process can match
the slowly executed plates of Mantegna, Marc
Antonio Ramondi, Albrecht Dürer, or Nanteuil
— who engraved after his own designs? From

the finesse of the Behams to the majestic sweep of Bervic, or the virtuosity of Antoine Masson — consider his head of Brisacier, the Gray-Haired Man — has not every manner, every mood, every technique been reproduced—rather, let us say, interpreted — in the terms of line-engraving? The engraved plate can state as succinctly as the etched the linear fretwork and silhouette of forms. Among other resources, the engraved plate is a method of the disposing of mass. It is more subtle than mezzotint in the indication of character, and is seldom so monotonous; while to the impressionism and often insignificant patterns of etching it opposes a static quality, opposes with its synthetic qualities of the permanent, the majestic, the gracious, and the powerful. As a medium it is as supple as either etching or scraped copper, though in this attribute it yields to wood-engraving.

What cannot line-engraving do in the way of interpretation? Think of the variety of technical styles and artistic individualities. Ambushed behind every laboriously engraved "steel" plate — steel is only in use since 1820 — there lurks a personality. Think of Mantegna, a master of line in his painting; of Lucas, of the quaint Martin Schongauer, of Altdorfer, Wierix — who aped Rembrandt in his version of The Three Trees — of Sadeler and Goltzius; of Caracci, Wille, Nanteuil, Raphael Morghen, Visscher, with his Sleeping Cat and his Rat-Catcher; of the Drevets, of William Sharp,

Robert Strange, and Woolet, the English trio; and George Friedrich Schmidt is still a name to conjure with. A litany of names might be recited of engravers who have made masterpieces. To-day, when we are in such a hurry to go nowhere to see nothing, the lenten and aristocratic art of line-engraving has lost its glamour, its significance. Nevertheless, a beautiful art it will always remain, beautiful notwithstanding the fluctuations of fashion. We feel that the pendulum of popular taste will surely swing back to this method of black-and-white, despite its slow, painful process of production. After an optical debauch in color, line is regaining its old supremacy. What else meant the apparition of cubism but a revolt against a too fluid impressionism! If this be true of easel-paintings it will come truer of line-engraving. The Sisters Five should walk abreast, not processionally — line, mezzotint, etching, wood-cutting and lithography are their names. And no one of this family is handsomer, more stately, more decorative, less "spotty" on a wall than the classics of line-engraving.

NEW RUSSIA FOR OLD

A DISTINGUISHED Russian diplomat, a visitor now in America, has asked us not to judge Russia too hastily; above all, not to abandon hopes for her future. The deposition of the Romanovs could not be accomplished without a social cataclysm and the presence of what Nicholas Murray Butler has so happily called "an inverted autocracy," that is to say, contemporary Bolshevikism. But the newcomers, after tumbling over thrones and dynasties, cannot be expected to halt at any half-way house of outworn political expediency. Their slogan is: All or Nothing. Everything is permitted. Precisely the device on the victorious standards of that strange Old Man of the Mountain, from whose followers we derive the sinister word "Assassin." Yet we are fain to believe that, as nothing long endures, the tremendous Russian muddle will be straightened out sometime. In the bad old days when the Russian moujik was not singing songs saturated with vodka, he spun legends shot through with the fantastic or grim with the pain of life. In the European concert his formidable bass voice made the voices of his neighbors seem thin and piping. Napoleon prophesied that before the end of the nineteenth century Europe would be either republican or

cossack, and a Moscow journal has proclaimed
that the "twentieth century belongs to us."
One need not be a Slavophile to admire Russian
patriotism. The love of a Russian for his country is a veritable passion. And from lips parched
by the desire of liberty, though the Russian be
persecuted, exiled, imprisoned, and murdered,
this passion is ever voiced with unabated intensity. What eloquent apostrophes have their
great writers made to their native land! The
youngest among the great nations, herself a nation with genius, she must possess a mighty
power thus to arouse the souls of her children.
How Turgénieff praised her noble tongue: "O!
mighty Russian language!" . . .

Yet the Russian is a cosmopolitan man; he is
more French than the Parisian, and a sojourner
among English ideas. Ivan Turgénieff, a Musco-
vite doubled by a Greek artist, was called a cosmopolitan by Dostoievsky — that profound and
sombre soul — and it was a frequent reproach
made during his lifetime that the music of
Tschaikovsky was not sufficiently national;
whereas to western ears it once smacked too
much of the Kalmuck. Naturally, Anton Rubinstein suffered from the same criticism; too
German for the Russians, too Russian for the
Germans. The case of Modeste Moussorgsky
is altogether different. If Russian music, the
organized musical speech of the nation, owes
much to Schumann, Berlioz, and Liszt, nevertheless Michael Glinka was its father. Like

Weber, he lovingly plucked from his native soil its wild flowers of melody, and gave them an operatic setting in his Ruslan and Life for the Czar. In his turn and representing the elder school are Darjomisky and Serov, while with New Russia blazoned on their banners follow César Cui, Rimsky-Korsakov, Borodin, Balikirev, Glazounov, Stcherbatchev, Rachmaninov, Arensky, Moussorgsky, and, last not least, Scriabin.

It might prove interesting to compare the cosmopolitanism of Tschaikovsky with Turgénieff's. George Moore insists with Celtic obstinacy that Turgénieff is the greatest master of fiction, greater even than Flaubert, because his art is effortless. Certainly, the Russian is the most artistic among novelists. Tschaikovsky was suspiciously regarded by the lesser native choir, while the big men, Gogol, Pushkin, Dostoievsky, and Tolstoy had an army of imitators, who wore their blouses untucked in their trousers. It was a symbol. Their watchword was: We are going to the People! From the Intelligentsia, the students, to the peasant himself, this ominous cry was heard. It is still sounded. Its echoes are in Western ears. The Great White Czar would not heed the warning. Going to the People is a phrase indicating a savage reaction against cosmopolitan influences; Russia had successively suffered from the invasions of English, French, and German ideas, customs, manners, costumes. The rabid Slavophilist would have none of these. He disliked Italian pictures, loathed German philosophy, despised French literature, and hated English politics. Yet, from these seemingly disparate elements was born a national consciousness, a national culture. Its eclecticism caused its disintegration.

To comprehend latter-day Russian music we should remember that the national spirit pervades its masterpieces. And that spirit is not in a special compartment separated from the seven arts, but waters their roots. With us art is a tender flower, isolated as if in a hothouse. The artist in America lives in a vacuum, or else creates his own atmosphere. In Russia, "barbarous" Russia, as we condescendingly refer to her, an artist is first a patriot. The English critic, John M. Robertson, wrote in 1891: "In that strange country where brute power seems to be throttling all the highest life of the people . . . there yet seems to be no cessation in the production of truthful literary art, . . . for justice of perception, soundness and purity of taste, and skill of workmanship, we in England with all our freedom, can offer no parallel." Tyranny, then, may be forcing ground for genius! From Gogol to Artzibachev Russian literature achieved its spiritual freedom despite the Czar and Siberia. The reason we speak of these writers and composers is because to know them is to grasp the psychology of Russian music, which is so often inspired by the poems, novels, and dramas of Pushkin, Lermontov, Gogol, Dostoievsky,

Turgénieff, Tolstoy, Ostrovsky, Gorky, Andrey-
ev, Artzibachev, and by the paintings of Repin,
Perov, Verestchagin, and, in the case of Prokofieff, by Boris Anisfeld.

We have elsewhere made a critical comparison
of Dostoievsky with Moussorgsky; no need to
refer to it here, except to say that when Dostoievsky wrote, "The soul of another is a dark
place, and the Russian soul is a dark place,"
he accurately plotted his nation's psychic curve.
And let it be said in passing that the author of
Crime and Punishment had developed the mystic idea (your Russian is nothing if not mystical)
that from Russia must come the salvation of the
peoples of the earth — from Russian Christianity. This notion became an obsession of the
great-souled writer, in whose Karamasov
Brothers and The Possessed (Besi), may be found
the leading motives of Nietzsche's philosophy:
the superman, the eternal recurrence, the fantastic idea that eternity may be in a "boxed-in"
bathhouse, an idea that Henri Barbusse, who is
saturated with Dostoievsky, develops in L'Enfer,
that infinity is contained within us. Eternity
is Now. Tolstoy, who was best described by
Count Melchior de Vogué in his epigram as
having "the mind of an English chemist in the
soul of a Hindoo Buddhist" ("On dirait l'esprit
d'un chimiste anglais dans l'âme d'un buddhiste
hindou") has not played as influential a rôle
among Russian composers because he was essentially tone-deaf. His Kreutzer Sonata demon-

strates how a man ignorant of music, great artist that he is, may write himself down absurdly. In comparison Dostoievsky is a spiritual reservoir of musical certitudes; while in Turgénieff, thanks to a natural sensibility and years of musical cultivation while sojourning in the household of the Viardot-Garcias at Paris — surely the happiest as well as the most artistic "ménage à trois" in history — he wrote of the art with sympathy and understanding.

The further one dives into the Orient the more chromatic become the arts, especially the tonal art. The chromatic scale was once the shibboleth of the Neo-Russian composer, and, being the artistic offspring of Liszt and the Slav, he vainly sought to veil his paternity by painting it over with local color. It was then a trackless and seldom explored country his, full of yawning harmonic precipices, melodies that are at once heavenly and hideous — like the mouth of a pretty woman with missing front teeth; mountainous ideals, bleak surprises, and rugged vistas. To-day matters have changed. The younger generation, headed by the astonishing Alexander Scriabin, has thrown chromaticism to the dogs. The whole-tone scale is monarch. Arnold Schoenberg declared the scale must escape the House of Bondage and be free from scholastic shackles. Modulation is to be as Free Love, which may supersede marriage — according to the recent programme of the Reds. Rebikov, Stravinsky, Serge Prokofieff, and Leo Ornstein have long ago nailed their color to the mast. It is unequivocally scarlet. Notwithstanding the seeming anarchy in all these social and artistic manifestations, we believe that to the Slav is the future. Out of darkest Russia may emerge the next world-composer. Scriabin may be only the Precursor of the new evangel. Dostoievsky is right. There is enough fire of righteousness in the Russians to burn up the world and all its wickedness. Russia is the matrix heavy with unborn genius, and who shall bear down too heavily now on her sorrow and travail? Water seeks its level. A country is no greater than her great men. And how truly great are those we have just named! New lamps for old. A new and glorious Russia for the old. Avos!

CEZANNE

CEZANNE was pre-eminently occupied with the problem of space and its corollaries, bulk, weight, density, and with the still more stupendous problem of getting on a flat surface the suggestion of a third dimension — thickness. To achieve even a suggestion proves him a genius. And he was a genius. His supreme technical qualities are volume, ponderability, and a personal color-scheme. What's the use of asking whether he is a sound draftsman or not? He is a master of "edges," a magician of tonalities. Huysmans spoke to me of the defective eyesight of Cézanne; but disease boasts its discoveries as well as health. Possibly his "abnormal" vision gave him glimpses of a reality denied to other painters. He advised students to look for the contrasts and correspondences of tone. He practised what he preached. No painter was so little affected by personal moods, by those variations of temperament dear to the professional artist. Did Cézanne possess the temperament he was always talking about? If he did, his temperament was not precisely decorative or flamboyant.

An unwearying experimenter, he seldom "finished" a picture. His morose landscapes were usually painted from one scene near his home at Aix. I saw the spot. The pictures do not closely resemble it — that is, in the photographic sense — which simply means that Cézanne had the vision and I had not. A few themes with polyphonic variations filled his simple life; art was submerged by its apparatus. His was the centripetal, not the centrifugal, temperament. In the domain of his rigid, intense ignorance there was little space for climate, charm, hardly for sunshine. Recall the blazing blue sky and sun of Provence, the tropical riot of its vegetation, its gamuts of green and scarlet, and then search for this mellow richness and misty, golden air in the pictures of the master. You won't find them in his dim, muffled surfaces, though a mystic light permeates his landscapes. It is the sallow-sublime in its apotheosis. He did not paint portraits of Provence as did Daudet in Numa Roumestan, or Bizet in L'Arlésienne. Cézanne sought for profounder meanings. The superficial, the facile, the staccato, the merely brilliant repelled him. Not that he was an "abstract" painter — as the self-contradictory atelier jargon goes. He was eminently concrete. He plays a legitimate "trompe-l'œil" on the optic nerve. His is not a pictorial illustration of Provence, but the slow, cruel delineation of a certain hill on old Mother Earth which exposes her bare torso, her bald, rocky pate and gravelled feet. The hallucination is inescapable.

As drab as the orchestration of Brahms, as austere in linear economy and as analytical as

Stendhal or Ibsen, the art of Cézanne never becomes truly lyric except in his still life. Upon an apple he lavishes his palette of smothered jewels. And, as all things are relative, an onion to him may be as beautiful as a naked woman. Taste is not one of his marked traits. The chiefest misconception of Cézanne is that of the theoretical fanatics who not only proclaim him chief of a school, which he is, but declare him to be the greatest painter since the Byzantines. This assertion I have read in cold type. There is a lot of inutile talk about "significant form" by propagandists — usually rotten bad painters. As if form had not always been "significant." When the impressionists as a school, now out-moded as the Barbizons, began to issue their prospectuses, the emphasis was laid upon form; form having served its purpose must go — at least become subordinate to color and its de-composition. The suave line of Raphael had degenerated into the insipid arabesques of Lefebvre, Bouguereau, and Cabanel. No deny-ing these truths, since become platitudes. Form is again in the ascendant, impressionism having in its turn become deliquescence. No one denies Cézanne's preoccupation with form, nor Cour-bet's, either. Consider the Ornan's landscapes, with their sombre flux of forest, painted by the crassest realist among French artists, though he seems hopelessly romantic to our sharper, more petulant mode of envisaging the world; yet what better example of "significant form" and solid structural sense than Courbet's? Nevertheless, Cézanne quite o'ercrows Courbet in his feeling for the massive — sometimes you can't see the ribs of his landscapes because of the skeleton.

Cézanne's was a twilight soul. And a humorless one. His early painting was quasi-structural, well-nigh modelling. Always the architectural sense. His rhythms are often elliptical. He has a predilection for the asymmetrical. Yet he is a man who lent to an art of two dimensions, the illusion of a third. His tactile values are raised to the nth degree. His color is personal. Huysmans was clairvoyant when, a half century ago, he wrote of Cézanne's work as containing the prodromes of a new art. The handling of his material alone absorbed him, and not its lyric, dramatic, anecdotic, or rhetorical elements. He despised "literary" painting. His portraits are charged with character. But he sometimes profoundly ponders unimportant matters — loses himself in a desert of sandy theorizing.

The tang of the town is not in his portraits of places. His leaden, metallic landscapes seldom spontaneously arouse to activity the jaded retina fed on Fortuny, Monticelli, or Monet. In his groups of bathing women there is no sex appeal. Merely women in their natural pelt, as heavy flanked as Percheron mares. They are as ugly as the females of Degas, and twice as truthful. With beauty, academic or operatic, he had no traffic. If you don't care for his graceless nudes, you may console yourself with the axiom that there is no disputing tastes — with the tasteless. We have seen some of his still-life pieces so acid in tonal quality as to suggest that divine dissonance produced on the palate by a stale oyster, or akin to the rancid note of an oboe in a pantomime score by Stravinsky. But what thrice subtle sonorities, what opulent color-chords may be found in his compositions. His fruits savor of the earth. Chardin interprets still-life with realistic beauty; when he paints an onion it reveals a certain grace. Vollon dramatizes it, or embroiders its homely shape with luxuriant decorations. When Cézanne paints an onion you smell it. His apples are — seemingly — falling off the table. How despairing are the efforts of his imitators to get those slanting surfaces covered with fruit and vegetables that have just been brought in by the cook. You say, Miraculous! and make a gesture to prevent the ripe stuff from sliding to the floor. The "representation" abhorred of the Cubists in its most pregnant shapes is there.

Cézanne did not occupy himself, as did Manet, with the ideas, manners and aspects of his generation. With the classic retort of Manet, he could have replied to those who taunted him with not "finishing" his pictures, "Sir, I am not a historical painter." Nor need we be disconcerted in any estimate of him by the depressing snobbery of collectors who don't know B from bull's foot but go off at half-trigger in their enthusiasm when a hint is dropped as to the possibilities of a painter appreciating in a pecuniary sense. Cézanne is the painting idol of the present crowd, as were Manet and Monet a few decades ago. These æsthetic fluctuations should not distract us. Henner, Cabanel, Bourguereau too, were idolized once upon a time and served to make a millionaire's holiday by hanging in his marble bathroom. It is the undeniable truth that Cézanne has, in the eyes of the younger generation, become a tower of strength which intrigues critical fancy. Cézanne is sincere to the core, yet even stark sincerity does not, of necessity, imply the putting forth of masterpieces. Before he attained his synthetic power he patiently studied Delacroix, Courbet, and the early Italians. At times he achieved the foundational structure of Courbet, though I don't think he had either the brains or the painting temperament of his elder contemporary, whose portée was at times tremendous. Hostile critics declare that the canvases of St. Paul of Provence are sans composition, sans linear pattern, sans personal charm. However, "popularity is for dolls," says Emerson.

I saw at the Champs de Mars Salon of 1901 a large picture by Maurice Denis, entitled Hommage à Cézanne, the idea of which was manifestly inspired by Manet's Hommage à Fantin-Latour, or Fantin's Batignolle School. The Maurice Denis canvas depicts a still-life by Cézanne on a chevalet, which is surrounded by

the figures of certain painters — Bonnard, Denis,
Redon, Roussel, Serusier, Vuillard, Mellério, and
Vollard. Cézanne is posed standing and is apparently embarrassed, which was his natural
condition. There was a special Cézanne Salle,
as there was one devoted to Eugene Carrière,
but Cézanne held the place of honor. With all
his naïve vanity he was dazzled by the uproarious
championship of "les jeunes," and, to give him
credit for a peasant astuteness, he was rather
suspicious of the demonstration. But he stolidly
accepted the frantic homage of the youngsters,
all the while looking like a bourgeois Buddha.
To-day a Cézanne of quality is costly. Why
not? When juxtaposed with many modern
painters his vital art makes other pictures seem
linoleum or papier maché. The nervous, shrink-
ing man I saw at Aix and later at Paris would
have been astounded at the praise printed since
his death; while he yearned for the publicity of
the official Salon — as did his school-friend Zola
for a seat in the Academy — none the less, he
disliked notoriety. He loved hard work. He
loved his solitude. With a fresh batch of canvases he trudged every morning to his pet landscape, the Motive, he called it, and it was there
that he daily slaved with genuine technical
heroism. When I first saw him he was a queer,
sardonic old gentleman in ill-fitting clothes, with
the shrewd, suspicious gaze of a provincial no-
tary. Like John La Farge, he hated shaking
hands. A rare impersonality.

Goethe has told us that because of his limitations we may recognize a master. The limitations of Cézanne are patent. An investigator, experimenter, even fumbler, he did not deem it wise to stray from his chosen, if narrow, field. His non-conformism defines his genius. Imagine reversing musical history and finding Johann Sebastian Bach following Richard Strauss. The very notion is monstrous. Yet, figuratively speaking, this order constitutes the case of Cézanne. He arrived on the pictorial scene after the classic, romantic, impressionistic, and symbolic schools. He is a primitive, not made like Puvis de Chavannes, but one born with an unaffected crabbed simplicity. Paul Cézanne will be remembered as a painter who respected his material, also as a painter, pure, without preoccupation in schools or ideas. No man who wields a brush need ask for a more enduring epitaph.

EILI EILI LOMO ASOVTONI?

"How shall we sing the Lord's song in a strange land?" I couldn't help recalling these words of the Psalmist, these and the opening, "By the rivers of Babylon," in which is compressed the immemorial melancholy of an enslaved race, when I heard Sophie Braslau intone with her luscious contralto, a touching Hebrew lament, "Eili Eili Lomo Asovtoni?" at a concert last winter. Naturally I believed the melody to be the echo of some tribal chant sung in the days of the Babylonian captivity, and perhaps before that in the days of the prehistoric Sumerians and the epic of Gilgamesh. Others have made the same error. Judge of my surprise when in a copy of *The American Jewish News* I read that the composer of Eili Eili is living, that his name is Jacob Kopel Sandler, that he wrote the music for a historical drama, Die B'ne Moishe (The Sons of Moses), which deals with the Chinese Jews. Mr. Sandler had written the song for Sophie Carp, a Yiddish actress and singer. The Sons of Moses was a failure, and a new piece, Brocha, the Jewish King of Poland, was prepared. (Not alluding to Pan Dmowski.) It was produced at the Windsor Theatre in the Bowery. The song, not the play, was a success. Then the music drifted into queer company, for music is a living organism and wanders when it is not controlled. Finally Sophie Braslau got hold of it, and the composer, who was directing a choir in a Bronx synagogue, was astounded to hear of the acclamations of a Metropolitan Opera House Sunday night audience. His daughter has listened to Eili Eili and brought home the good news. After troublesome preliminaries "Meyer Beer," the pen name of the musical editor of *The American Jewish News*, was able to prove beyond peradventure of a doubt the artistic parentage of the song, and Jacob Sandler is in a fair way of being idolized in his community, as he should be.

Eili Eili lomo asovtoni? may be found in Psalm 22, the first line of the second verse in Hebrew. In the English version the words of David are in the first verse: "My God, my God, why hast thou forsaken me?" And in the St. Mark's Gospel we read: "And at the ninth hour Jesus cried with a loud voice, saying, 'Eloi, Eloi, lama sabachthani?' which is, being interpreted: 'My God, my God, why hast thou forsaken me?'" (Chapter 15, verse 34.) The exegetists and apologists, as well as sciolists, have made of this immortal phrase a bone of theological contention. Schmiedel, who with Harnack believes the words to have been uttered by our Saviour, nevertheless points out various details which prefigure the same things in the crucifix — the just man hanging on the stake, the perforated hands and feet, the mocking crowd, the soldiers gambling for the clothes, everything takes place as described in the Psalm. Lublinski (in Dogma, p. 93) and Arthur Drews (in The Historicity of Jesus, p. 150) demur to the orthodox Christian conclusions of Harnack and Schmiedel. A beloved master, the late Solomon Schechter, disposed of the question in his usual open style. "The world is big enough," he has said to me, for both Jehovah and Jesus, "for two such grand faiths as the Hebrew and the Christian." But he saw Christianity only in its historical sequence, and not as a continuator of Judaism; rather, a branching away from the main trunk. If it had not been for Constantine, the world might be worshipping Mithra to-day, was the erudite and worthy man's belief. Enveloped in the mists of the first two centuries Christianity seems to have had a narrow escape from the doctrines of Mithraism. That Salomon Reinach practically admits in his Orpheus, a most significant study of comparative religions from the pen of this French savant.

Once upon a time I played the organ in a "shool," a reformed, not an orthodox, synagogue; played indifferently well. But my acquaintance with the Jewish liturgy dates back to my boyhood in Philadelphia, where I studied Hebrew, in company with Latin. The reason? My mother fondly hoped that I might become a priest — the very thought of which makes me shudder now. The religious in me found vent in music, and my love of change was gratified by playing the Hebrew service on Shabbas (Saturday) and the Roman Catholic on our Sabbath. Probably that is why I was affected by Sophie Braslau's singing of Eili Eili. Rosa Raisa has put the song in her repertory, and only on Easter Sunday last did Sarah Borni sing it, although it appeared on the programme as a composition of Kurt Schindler's, an error quickly rectified by Miss Borni, who did not know the authorship till too late. "Such songs," commented this soprano, "come but once in a man's lifetime." Dorothy Jardon will no doubt sing Eili Eili, as she sang for the first time a Jahrzeit, a Kaddish by Rhea Silberta, at the Hippodrome last Sunday. Mr. Sandler has come into his own, and it is gratifying to record that the credit is largely due to Meyer Beer and *The American Jewish News*.

I have always entertained a peculiar admiration for the Jews and Judaism. It began with the study of Semitic literature of the Talmud, above all of Hebrew poetry, the most sublime in our language, as Matthew Arnold asserts in his comparative estimate of Greek and Hebraic cultures. My dearest friends have been, still are, of that race. Prejudice, social or political, against the Jew, I not only detest, but I have never been able to comprehend. My early playmates were Jewish boys and girls. I have stood under the "Choopah" (marriage canopy), and have seen many a Bar-Mitzvah; even sat "Shivah" for the dead father of intimate friends.

EILI EILI LOMO ASOVTONI?

From Rafael Joseffy to Georg Brandes; from the brilliant Hungarian virtuoso that was Joseffy — whose father, a learned rabbi, I visited at Budapest — in Pest-Ofen — in 1903, when he was eighty-four, an Orientalist, a linguist with twenty-six languages, ancient and modern, at the tip of his tongue — to Professor Brandes, the Danish scholar, an intellectual giant, and a critic in the direct line of Sainte-Beuve and Taine — both men I knew and loved. Whether the Jew has attained the summits as a creator in the seven arts I cannot speak authoritatively, although the Old Testament furnishes abundant evidences that he has in poetry. Disraeli (Beaconsfield), who liked to tease Gladstone by calling him "Frohstein" and pointing to his rugged Jewish prophet's features, has written of his race most eloquently. I should like to quote a passage in its entirety, but time and space forbid. But an excerpt I permit myself the luxury of reproduction: "The ear, the voice, the fancy teeming with combinations, the inspiration fervid with picture and emotion, that came from Caucasus, and which we have preserved unpolluted, have endowed us with almost the exclusive privilege of music; that science of harmonious sounds which the ancients recognized as most divine and deified in the person of their most beautiful creation. . . ." He goes on: "There is not a company of singers, not an orchestra in a single capital, that is not crowded with our children under feigned names which they adopt to conciliate the dark aversion which your posterity will some day disclaim with shame and disgust. . . ."

Lord Beaconsfield mentions Rossini, Meyerbeer, Mendelssohn as Jewish composers, and Pasta and Grisi among the singers. Probably he had not heard Rossini's witticism uttered on his deathbed: "For heaven's sake, don't bury me in the Jewish cemetery!" Nor did Beaconsfield look far enough ahead when he wrote "dark aversion" — which is wonderful. To-day the boot is on the other leg. It may be Gentiles who will be forced to change their names to Jewish. I could easily sign myself "Shamus Hanuchah" — leaving out the "lichts" — or pattern after the name Paderewski jokingly wrote on his photograph: "For Jacob Hunekerstein."

And I am ashamed to confess that I know Jews who themselves are ashamed of having been born Jews. Incredible! In Vienna I have seen St. Stefan's Cathedral crowded at the 11 o'clock high mass by most fervent worshippers, the majority of whom seemed Semitic, which prompted me to propound the riddle: When is a Jew not a Jew? Answer: When he is a Roman Catholic in Vienna. But you never can tell. As Joseffy used to say when some musician with a nose like the Ten Commandments was introduced, as, for example, Monsieur Fontaine, "He means Brunnen, or, in Hebrew, Pischa. He is not a Jew, but his grandmother wore a 'scheitel'" (the wig still worn by orthodox Jewish women). The truth is that among the virtuosi, singers, actors, the Jew holds first place. Liszt and Paganini are the exceptions, and Paganini could easily pass in an east side crowd as Jehudah. As to the Wagner controversy, not started by Nietzsche, but by Rossini and Meyerbeer, who referred to Wagner as Jewish, that was settled by O. G. Sonneck in his little book, Was Wagner a Jew? but only after I had introduced to the columns of the *New York Times Sunday Magazine* in 1913, a book by Otto Bournot, entitled Ludwig Geyer. Geyer was, as you may remember, the stepfather of Richard Wagner. Bournot had access to the Baireuth archives and delved into the newspapers of Geyer's days. August Böttiger's Necrology had hitherto been the chief source. Mary Burrell's Life of Wagner was the first to give the true spelling of the name of Wagner's mother, which was Bertz, which may be Jewish or German, as you like.

The Geyers as far back as 1700 were pious folk. The first of the family mentioned in local history was a certain Benjamin Geyer, who about 1700 was a trombone player and organist. Indeed, the Geyers were largely connected with the evangelical church. Ludwig Geyer, virtually acknowledged by Baireuth as the real father of Richard Wagner, looked Jewish (which proves nothing, as I have seen dark, Semitic fisher-folk on the coast of Galway) and displayed Jewish versatility. For that matter the composer von

Weber looked like a Jew, as does Camille Saint-Saëns. When I ventured to write of this racial trait — much more marked in his youth — the French composer sent me a denial, sarcastically asking how a man with such a "holy" name as "Saint-Saëns" could be Jewish. But Leopold Godowsky, who was intimate with him, has told me that he took his mother's name. As to Wagner, a little story may suffice. In 1896 I attended the Wagner festival at Baireuth. Between performances I tramped the Franconian hills. My toes hurt me. Looking for a corn-cutter, I found one not far from the Wagner house. The old chap seated me in his doorway, probably to get better light, and as he crouched over my feet in the street I asked him if he had known Richard Wagner. "Know Wagner!" he irascibly replied. "He passed my shop every day. Many the times I cut his corns. Oh, no! not here; over yonder" — he jerked his head in the direction of Wahnfried. I inquired what kind of a looking man was Wagner. "He was a little bow-legged Jew, and he always wore a long cloak to hide his crooked legs." Enfin! the truth from the mouth of babes. This beats Nietzsche and his "Vulture" Geyer.

Not religion, not nationality, but race, counts in the individual. Wagner looked like a Jew. And there are many red-haired Jews with pug noses and light blue eyes. Renan in Le Judaisme has shown us how non-Jewish elements were in the course of time incorporated within the race.

The Chazars of eastern Europe are Jews, only a thousand years old. Dr. Brandes in a confession of his views on the subject has said — in *The Journal for Jewish History and Literature*, published at Stockholm (*Teldscript for Judisk Historia*), and quoted by Bernard G. Richards in a capital study of Brandes — "from the fifteenth to the sixteenth year of my life I regarded Judaism purely as a religion." But when he was abused as a Jew then Georg Brandes felt himself a genuine Jew. Many a man has found himself in a similar position. Atavistic impulses, submerged in subconsciousness, may explain why certain men, Gentiles, scholars, by nature noncombatants, have left their peaceful study, jeopardized their life, ruined their reputation, to battle for an obscure Jew Dreyfus. Zola, of Greek-Levantine origin, perhaps Italian and Jew, was one of those valiant souls who fought for the truth. Anatole France, born Thibault, another. Count Thibault, at the time of the Dreyfus uproar, challenged the great writer who signs himself Anatole France to prove his right to that distinguished Roman Catholic name. That the gentle Anatole is the very spit and spawn of a Jew, so far as appearance goes; that since Heine (baptized a Christian) no such union of mocking irony and tender, poetic emotion can be noted in the work of any writer, are alike valueless as testimony. Nevertheless, many believe in this Hebraic strain; just as they feel it in the subtlety of Cardinal Newman's writing — he was of Dutch stock — and in the humor of Charles Lamb. Both Englishmen are credited with the "precious quintessence," as Du Maurier would say.

I have had to stand a lot of good-natured fun poked at me for my Jewish propensity. I can stand it, as I have a solid substratum of history for my speculations. Some years ago *The Contemporary Review* printed an article entitled "The Jew in Music," with this motto from Oscar Wilde's Salome: "The Jews believe only in what they cannot see." The writer's name was signed: A. E. Keeton. Not even the assertion that Beethoven was a Belgian is half so iconoclastic as some of the assumptions made in this study. "When Mozart first appeared as a prodigy before the future Queen of France, Marie Antoinette, she announced that 'a genius must not be a Jew.' The original name, Ozart, was changed. Mozart was baptized! Which anecdote makes the scalp to freeze, though not because of its verisimilitude. Beethoven and Rubinstein looked alike; ergo! But then they didn't. In the case of Chopin he was certainly Jewish-looking, especially in the Winterhalter and Kwiatowski portraits. His father came from Nancy, in Lorraine, thickly populated by Jews. The original name, Szopen, or Szop, is Jewish. His music, especially the first Scherzo in B minor, has a Heine-like irony, and irony is a prime characteristic of the Chosen (or Choosing as Zangwill puts it) race! But all this is in the

key of wildest surmise. Wagner was born in
the ghetto at Leipsic; yet that didn't make him
Jewish, any more than the baptism of Mendelssohn made him Christian. Georges Bizet was
of Jewish origin, he looked Jewish; but the fact
that he married the daughter of Halévy (Ha-
Levi), the composer of La Juive, didn't make the
composer of Carmen a Jew. Neither religion
nor nationality are any more than superficial
factors in the nature of men and women. Race
alone counts.

Once upon a time I wrote a Jewish story,
The Shofar Blew at Sunset. Maggie Cline
liked it; so did Israel Zangwill. I preserve a
letter from Mr. Zangwill telling me of his liking.
The story appeared in M'lle New York, now defunct. It was afterward translated into Yiddish, though it did not give general satisfaction
in either camp, Jewish or Christian. It revelled
in the cantillations and employed as leading motive the Shofar, or ram's-horn blown in the syna-
gogues on Yom Kippur or the Day of Atonement.
The scroll of the Torah also appeared. But these
liturgical references didn't offend; it was my surprising denunciation of Jewish materialism in
New York that was the rock of offence. I say
surprising, for what is a Christian-born doing in
another field and finding fault? I'm sure I
can't say why, unless that in writing the tale I
unconsciously dramatized myself as a reproach-
ing voice. There was much in my strictures of
that son of Hanan who prowled through the

streets of the Holy City in the year A. D. 62, crying aloud: "Woe, woe upon Jerusalem!" I remember that I predicted because of the luxury of the American Jew the lofty Jewish idealism might be submerged in a flood of indifference and disbelief. Prosperity would prove the snag. In the heart of the Jew is the true Zion, not in success nor in some far-away land. Naturally, that didn't please the Zionists. One professional Jewish publication, no longer in existence, said that I preached like a Rabbi (Reb), but thought like a goi. The word "Chutzpah" was also used. Yet, wasn't I right? It is the spiritual Ark of the Covenant, the spirit of the law, and not the letter that killeth, which should be enshrined in the heart of the Jew. He may dream of Palestine, of its skies of the "few large stars," a land overflowing with milk and honey; but in the depths of his soul it is the living God to whom he must go for spiritual sustenance. God the eternal reservoir of our earthly certitudes! Schma' Ysroel!

SOCIALISM AND MEDIOCRITY

In these piping times of peace when the body politic is afflicted with socialism, bolshevism, and other cutaneous disorders, it is a pleasing and a profitable task to reread Socialistic Fallacies, by M. Yves Guyot, who for years has been a determined and consistent opponent of the bleak and dismal "science" and the author of a number of books on the subject. Luckily for those who can't read French, Socialistic Fallacies has been translated and should prove a manual to combat and confute the sophistries of socialism with the writer's arsenal of arguments. M. Guyot has been a deputy, a municipal councillor, minister of public works. He advocated the revision of the Dreyfus case, and he was political editor of Le Siècle (1892–1903). He is also editor of Journal des Economistes (since 1909) and editor of L'Agence Economique et Financières (since 1911). He has written much about the great war and its causes (also translated) and kindred themes. Therefore a man who knows what he is talking about.

In his drastic attack on socialistic fallacies he thus concludes: "There are three words which socialism must erase from the façades of our public buildings, the three words of the republican motto: Liberty, Equality, Fraternity. Liberty, because socialism is a rule of tyranny; equality, because it is a rule of class; fraternity, because its policy is that of class war." M. Guyot might have quoted Napoleon, a realist, a cynic in politics, for he knew its seamy side, who said: "Tell men they are equal and they won't bother about liberty." And in this matter men may change, mankind never.

Socialism, that word of so many meanings, has itself become meaningless. Guyot shows us each variety, analyzes its particular fallacy, and though not a victim to the craze for statistics, he furnishes many pages of figures to match those of his adversaries. He attacks Karl Marx on his weakest flank, and, incidentally, proves him not to have been a proletarian, but the son-in-law of a Prussian Junker. The selfishness of Marx, his tyrannical behavior, his unphilosophical wrath when opposed by two such intellectual giants as Bakunine and Lassalle; his jealous attitude toward Ferdinand Lassalle, especially after his tragic death, are all well known. These traits do not reveal a man overflowing with true brotherly love. Able, but frequently unscrupulous, men amuse the idle and attract the multitude — such are the leaders of the cause which has made such headway in Germany, adds Guyot, whose words in the light of contemporaneous history are positively prophetic. These leaders are plagiarists, with some variations, of all the communist romances originally inspired by Plato. Their greatest pundits, Marx and

Engels, have built up their theories upon a sentence of Saint-Simon and three phrases of Ricardo's. Our author gives these examples: "German socialism is derived from two sources: (1) The French doctrine of Saint-Simon, 'The way to grow rich is to make others work for one,' which in Proudhon's mouth becomes 'the exploitation of man by man.' (2) Three formulas of Ricardo, viz.: (a) labor is the measure of value; (b) the price of labor is that which provides the laborer in general with the means of subsistence, and of perpetuating his species without either increase or diminution; (c) profits decrease in proportion as wages increase." Formula (b) became the "iron law of wages" enunciated by Lassalle. Inverted dogmatism all these stale subterfuges.

The French doctrines and Ricardo's three formulas were transformed into the theory of Rodbertus, "the normal time of labor," and the "surplus labor" theory of Karl Marx and Engels. Guyot calmly demonstrates the fallacies of these sonorous assumptions. He asks the whereabouts of the Utopias of Fourier, of Cabet, of Louis Blanc's organization of labor, or of Proudhon's bank of exchange — that Proudhon who has been permanently saddled with Brissot's famous phrase: "Property is theft." (Philosophical Examination of Property and Theft, 1780.) No Socialist has succeeded in explaining the conditions for the production, the remuneration, and the distribution of capital in a collectivist system. No Socialist has succeeded in determining the motives for action which an individual would obey. When pressed for an answer, they allege that human nature shall be metamorphosed, but that the individual remains a constant quantity! Rank materialism all this, and absolutely without vision.

Socialism is a hierarchy on a military basis imported from Germany. Karl Marx did not concern himself with the incentives to action which are to be placed before men in communistic society, and his followers carefully evade the question. When they do attempt to deal with it, they fall into grotesque errors, as did the late French leader, Jaurès. Kautsky asks how the workman is to be made to take an interest in his work, and he can find no incentive other than the force of habit. Like mechanical toys, men will do the same thing every day because they did it the day before. This is merely teaching tricks to animals, the organization of reflex action causing the individual mechanically to do to-morrow what he did yesterday. Nor is this a discovery of scientific socialism; the organizers of churches, of armies, discovered the trait long ago, employing it as a means of discipline under the sanctions of allurement and coercion; allurement, by preferments, decorations, and honorary distinction; coercion, by means of more or less cruel and rigorous punishments. Bebel declared that "a man who will not work has not the right to eat." This is being condemned to death by starvation; and a man who does less work than, in the opinion of the executive, he ought to do, shall be put upon a restricted diet; so, after all, the collectivist ideal ends in servile labor. To replace a king or a president there will be an "executive," which means several instead of one tyrant. Good old King Log is always a better ruler than King Stork. For one thing, he is not so voracious as the ferociously hungry feathered biped. Socialism, then, is only one more strait-jacket to torture the individual.

It may be said that man is ready for every form of sacrifice save one: nowhere and at no time has he been found to labor voluntarily and constantly from a disinterested love for others. Man is only compelled to productive labor by necessity, by the fear of punishment, or by suitable remuneration. The Socialists of to-day, like those of former times, constantly denounce the waste of competition. Competition involves losses, but biological evolution, as well as humanity, proves that they are largely compensated by gain. Furthermore, there is no question of abolishing competition in socialistic conceptions; the question is merely one of the substitution of political for economic competition. If economic competition leads to waste, and claims its victims, it is none the less productive. Political competition has secured enormous plunder to great conquerors, such as Alexander, Cæsar, Tamerlane, and Napoleon; it always destroys more wealth than it confers upon the victor. The Socialist formulates a theory of robbery and calls it "restitution to the disinherited." Disinherited by whom? Disinherited of what? Let them produce their title-deeds! They call it expropriation, but that is a misnomer; what they set out to practise is confiscation. Georges Bernard says that "socialism will be a régime of authority." On this point Guyot grimly agrees with him. In reality it will be the most oppressive spiritual and material system ever invented by man.

Socialist action has a depressing effect on all fixed capital, and, he continues, "in order to carry on a policy of preserving the political equilibrium, of giving a few bones to the demagogues to gnaw, concessions are made to the policy of spoliation." What, then, remains of socialism when we come to close quarters with it? And what are the prospects of this spoliation and tyranny? The socialistic party cannot balance up a governmental majority without destroying government itself, for it cannot admit that government fulfils the minimum of its duties (this was written before 1914). When a strike breaks out the intention of the strikers is that security of person and property shall not be guaranteed. Socialist policy represents contempt for law, and all men, whether rich or poor, have an interest in liberty, security, and justice, as the private interest of each individual is bound up with these common blessings. But

Socialists despise them all. "The socialism of Karl Marx's disciples betrays a long apprenticeship to servitude," declares M. Reinach.

A law, the object of which is to protect each man's property, is supported by all who possess anything, and where is the man in advanced societies who is incapable of being robbed because he possesses nothing?

A law of spoliation may be passed and carried into effect, but in the event of its results becoming permanent it runs the risk of destroying the government which has assumed the responsibility of it. Socialist policy is a permanent menace to the liberty and security of citizens, and, therefore, cannot be the policy of any government, the primary duty of which is to exact respect for internal and external security. If it fail therein it dissolves and is replaced by anarchy; and, inasmuch as every one has a horror of that condition, which betrays itself by the oppression of violent men banded together solely by their appetites, an appeal is made to a strong government and to a man with a strong grip, and then the risk is incurred of relapsing into all the disgraces and disasters of Cæsarism. In several sections of this admirable work, M. Guyot scrutinizes the various Utopias from Plato to Proudhon: Sir Thomas More, the Kingdom of the Incas, Campanella, the Jesuits in Paraguay, Moselly, Robert Owen, Fourier, the American Phalanx, the Oneida Community, Cabet, the Icarians, and other unsuccessful experimenters. Utopia is always within sight, but never reached. It is, in the charming parlance of the hour, a pipe-dream; these Utopias always cut their throats to spite their thirst. And precisely where socialism was expected to be a buffer against world wars, it dismally failed.

From time to time the everlasting busybody asks himself why a plea for mediocrity is not a fitting theme to interest ambitious essayists. Supermen and supper-rogues have been done to the death in print, yet few words are accorded to the garden variety of the human plant. Instead we are keyed to the loftiest pitch; exaggeration is a national neurosis. We are all professional altruists, and, as every one knows, altruism is the art of making our neighbor unhappy because of our oppressive happiness. And yet not a word for mediocrity, which is the backbone of our nation, the staple of its political, artistic, and literary productions. Not a word for the man in the street, whose collective opinion — King Opinion, the most despotic of tyrants — rules us, whose vote counts heavier than the vote of the "exceptional" being perched on the housetop. (A majority of exalted souls would turn America into a wilderness.) And all because the excellent word "mediocrity" is become debased in meaning. At one time it stood for the golden mean, for a happy equilibrium of forces, moral and physical. It spelled happiness to its possessor — we refer to the mediocre temperament — and if a man had enough money to keep the wolf from the door he was content. That is the precise word — content; to be contented is a gift of the gods. But to us nowadays it means that you are merely commonplace, without social ambitions, without intellectual eminence. And this is not well.

Notwithstanding the fact that we are a united nation of over one hundred millions of people, we are each in his own fashion endeavoring to escape the imputation of mediocrity. Alas! in vain. Number is mediocrity. We think and drink to order, vote as we are bidden by our wives, and wear the clothes given us by destroyers of sartorial taste. Wherefore, then, this mad desire to be exceptional? Whence this optimism that shudders in the presence of genuine art and espouses the vulgar because it better agrees with fat nerves? Let us acknowledge the truth. It is because, happily for us, we are all mediocre; because genius is not a normal condition of humanity, and that talent is much less rare than our national vanity admits. However, let us pluck up courage. The future — which is said by some to belong to socialism — will work out the problem of mediocrity, especially if socialism is involved; mediocrity and socialism are not poles asunder. Concrete houses filled with people who will eat, drink, and think alike will cover the land. Everything will be of concrete, even our political opinions. In his concrete Capitol a concrete President will devise concrete laws. Art, music, and literature will be so concrete that our native Gradgrinds, hungry for hard facts, will be ravished into the seventh concrete heaven. Made a law, mediocrity will do away with our present mortifying doubts, deceptions, and pretensions. O Happy Time! And this coming age of concrete, wherein all must walk and look alike, is it not a dream compared with which Dante's Inferno would be a Garden of Armida?

Said a great poet-philosopher: "And many a man has gone into the desert and suffered from thirst with the camels rather than sit about the cistern with dirty camel drivers." No wonder William James wrote that "the whole atmosphere of present-day Utopian literature tastes mawkish and dish-watery to people who still keep a sense of life's more bitter flavors." And how much more that is insipid and mawkish will follow under socialistic regimentation! "Is it not the chief disgrace in the world not to be a unit; to be reckoned one character; not to yield that peculiar fruit which each man was created to bear, but to be reckoned in the gross, in the hundreds of thousands, of the party, of the section to which we belong, and our opinion predicted geographically as the North or the South?" These words were not uttered by a Socialist; they emanated from the crystal-clear intellect of our greatest Individualist, Ralph Waldo Emerson.

CHOPIN OR THE CIRCUS?

RATHER hotly I argued the question with my editor: "After all, music critics are men and brethren," I said. "Except when they are sisters," he ironically interposed. I sternly resisted a temptation to blush, and continued: "Because I love Chopin must I forever write of his music — toujours perdrix! It's an indigestion of strawberries, clotted cream, and green-eyes. I'm suffering from spring-fever. Let me write a story about the circus." "Why not Ibsen?" interposed my editor, who is subtle or nothing. "He was a grand man," I assented, "but in the present case he is only a red-herring across the trail. Suppose I mix up Chopin with sawdust merely for the sake of the mélange?" My chief assented, wearily. There are more important problems on the carpet than Chopin.

Had I ever been to the circus? What a singular question! Yet, yet—! No, I confessed to myself, I had not been to the circus for at least three decades. Critics are tame cats away from their regular guests. In the concert room or at the play, armed with our little hammers, we are as brave as plumbers; but on a roof garden, in church, at a circus, or innocently slumbering, we are the mildest gang of pirates that ever scut-

tled an American sonata or forced ambitious
leading ladies to walk the plank. We may go
alone to the theatre with impunity and another
fellow's girl, but at the circus we need a nurse
to show us the ropes and keep us from falling
under the elephants' hoofs. I know, because
I went one Sunday night to the Hippodrome
and liked John McCormack's singing immensely;
so much indeed that I forgot to criticise and
nearly fell over the edge of the box, so uncriti-
cally did I applaud. A private nurse — not
necessarily old — say I is the only safety for a
critic out of his element; otherwise a sense of
the dignity of our calling is not maintained.

Therefore, I swallowed my Chopin scheme
without undue fervor and went to the circus.
No matter which one. All circuses are in an
attractive key to me. Thackeray said the same
thing about the play, and said it better. Any
circus will serve as a peg for my sawdust symbolism. Any Garden will do, so that it has a
capitalized initial letter. (No allusion to Magical Mary.) The circus! What a corrective for
the astringent Ibsen or the morbidezza of Sar-
matia's sweet singer, Chopin! The circus! It
is a revelation. One thing I regretted — that I
could not be a boy again, with dirty hands, a
shining brow, and a heart brimming over with
joy. Peter Pan! Oh! to recapture that first
careless rapture, as Browning or some other
writing Johnny said; surely he must have meant
the circus, which is the one spot on our muddy

planet where rapture rhymes with the sawdust ring.

"Have you ever seen Hedda Gabler?" I asked of the Finland giantess. We were wedged in front of the long platform at the Garden, upon which were the Missing Link, the Snake-Enchantress, the Lion-Faced Boy, the English Fat Girl — so fat — the Human Skeleton, the Welsh Giant, the Lilliputians, tattooed men, a man with an iron skull, dancers, jugglers, gun-spinners, "lady" musicians, and the three-legged boy. Eternal types at the circus. The noise was terrific, the air dense with the aura of unwashed humanity. This aura was twin to the aura in a monkey house. But I enjoyed my "bath of multitude," as Charles Baudelaire names it, and I should not have bothered the tall creature with such an inept question. She coldly regarded me:

"No, I haven't seen Hedda to-day, but I remember George Tesman always teased her with one question, 'What do you know about that, Hed?' Shoo! Sardou for mine." "Do you read George Blarney Shaw?" I persisted. "He ought to be in a cage here. He would draw some crowds. But I'm told he lives in Germany now on account of the beer." I backed away quickly as an East Side family consisting of a baker's dozen, would allow. Why had I asked such a question of a perfect stranger? This giantess, I mused before the rhinoceros with the double prongs, is Finnish. That's why she knew

the name of Hedda Gabler. Why didn't I speak
of Rosmersholm? Rebecca West had Finnish
blood in her veins. Careful, careful — this
Ibsen obsession must be surmounted, else I shall
be inquiring of the giraffe if neck or nothing is
the symbol of Brand. All or Nothing! of course.
How stupid of me. Among the animals I re-
gained my equilibrium. Their odors evoked
memories. Yes, I recalled the old-time circus,
with its compact pitched canvas tent on North
Broad Street, Philadelphia: the pink lemonade,
the hoarse voice of the man who entreated us
to buy tickets — there were no megaphones in
those days — the crisp crackling of the roasting
peanuts, the ovens revolved by the man from
Ravenna, the man from Ascoli, and the man from
Milan. They followed the circus all the way
from Point Breeze, and I swear they were to me
far more human than the policemen who gently
whacked us with their clubs when we crawled
under the tent.

The sense of smell is first aid to memory.
As I passed the cages saluting our pre-Adamic
relatives, bidding the time of day to the zebu,
nodding in a debonair fashion to the yak, I
could not help longing for my first circus.
Again I saw myself sitting in peaceful agony on
a splintery plank; again I felt the slaps and
pinches of my tender-hearted Aunt Sue — now
in Paradise, I hope; again my heart tugged like
a balloon at its moorings as the clowns jumped
into the ring, grimacing, chortling, and fascinat-

ing us with their ludicrous inhumanity. Again
we sat, a lot of noisy rapscallions, on the stoop
of Edwin Forrest's home — the old Forrest man-
sion is still on the west side of Broad Street —
and how we tumbled to the sidewalk when that
terrific tragedian opened the door and trans-
fixed us with his glittering glance. I can still
see his leonine head with its shock of iron-gray
curls, his exposed bull-neck, and hear his angry
roar: "Get to blank out of here, you blankety-
blanks!" It was the giant's voice of Metamora,
Coriolanus, Lear that we heard, an echo from
the grand period in the history of the American
theatre; but we didn't know that. We were
mischievous boys, and made mock of the mighty
Edwin, no doubt adding insult to injury by
twiddling derisive thumbs at our noses.

Other days, other ways. I sighed as I tore
myself loose from the prehensile trunk of a too
friendly baby elephant and passed into the huge
auditorium where Gilmore had played. Ah!
the sad, bad, glad, dear, dead, tiresome, poverty-
stricken, beautiful days when we were young
imbeciles and held hands with a fresh "ideal"
every week (sometimes two). Ah! the sentimental "jag" induced by peanut eating, and
the chaste, odoriferous apes.

It is time. We seat ourselves. I look about
me. Two resplendent gentlemen wearing evening clothes at high noon, after the daring manner of our Gallic cousins, toll a bell. I became
excited. Why those three and thirty strokes?

What the symbolism! Chopin, or Ibsen; again,
I groaned, and turned my attention to my
neighbors, one of whom I could feel, though
did not see. I raised my voice, employing certain vocables hardly fit to print. The effect
was magical. "Johnny, take your feet out of
the gentleman's collar. That's a good boy."
It was the soothing voice of a mother. Bless her
clairvoyance! I sat comfortably back in my
seat. Johnny howled at the interference with
his pleasure. I felt sorrow for him. Childhood
is ever individualistic, even pragmatic. But I
only had one collar with me, and it was well the
matter thus ended.

Hurrah! Here they come! A goodly band.
The clowns! the clowns! Some hieratic owl of
wisdom has called the clown the epitome of mankind. He certainly stands for something, this
"full-fledged fool," as good old Tody Hamilton
used to write, and "surcharged with the Roe
of Fun," which phrase beats Delaware shad.
Odds fish! There was only one Hamilton.
What a Rabelaisian list of names boast these
merry clowns! If the years have passed over
the skulls of these lively rascals, jolly boys do
not show them. The same squeaks, the identical yodling, the funny yet sinister expression
of the eyes, the cruel, red-slitted mouths — not
a day older than ten did I seem as they came
tumbling in and began their horse-play, punctu-
ated with yelling, yahoo gestures, ribald ejacula-
tions, and knockabout diversions. It must all

mean something, this hooting, in the economy of the universe, else "life is a suck and a sell," as Walt Whitman puts it. As in a dream-mirror I saw Solness slowly mount the fatal tower when Hilda Wangel cries to him: "My — my Master-builder!" She sings The Maiden's Wish, and he hears the harps of Chopin hum in the air. I rub my ears. It is not Hilda who is crying, but a pet pig in a baby carriage, wheeled by a chalk-faced varlet. How difficult it is to escape the hallucinations of the critical profession. I couldn't forget Chopin or Ibsen even at the circus.

It was with relief, after more bellmanship from the man with the shiny silk hat and spiked coat, as the elephants majestically entered. Followed the horses. Tumblers and wire-walkers, women who stood on their heads and smiled — as they do in life. Something like the "inverted pyramid," as James Hinton called modern civilization — plastic poseurs, Oriental jugglers, the show was let loose at last. Human projectiles were launched through midair to the tap of a drum. My nerves forbade me to look at them, so I read a programme advertisement of wall-paper for bathrooms. Some people like such horrible sights. I do not. They dare not precisely formulate to themselves the wish that "something" would happen, and when it does they shudder with sadistic joy. I close my eyes when the Whirl of Death or any other sensational act is staged. "Something" might happen.

The mad dancers delight our rhythmic sense as they make marvellous arabesques. The chariot races stir the blood. The crash around curves, the patters of gleaming metal excite so that you stand up, and, brushing the feet of inevitable Johnny from your neck (notwithstanding his remonstrances), you shout with woolly mouth and husky voice. Instinctively you turn down your thumbs: "Pollice verso," which Bayard Taylor translated "the perverse police." You remember the Gérôme painting?

"This beats Ibsen," I hilariously exclaimed to Johnny's mother. (She was a comely matron.) "His name is John, and when he gets home his father will beat him," she tartly replied. With the prevoyance of boyhood Johnny burst into despairing howls. I at once folded up my mind. A million things were happening in the haze of the many rings. The New Circus is polyphonic, or nothing.

Enough! Filled to the eyes with the distracting spectacle, ear-drums fatigued by the blare and bang of the monster brass band, my collar quite wilted by Johnny's shoemaker, my temper in rags because of the panting, struggling army of fellow-beings, I reached the avenue in safety, perspiring, thirsty, unhappy. Like Stendhal, after his first and eagerly longed-for battle of love, I exclaimed: "Is that all?" In sooth, it had been too much. The human sensorium is savagely assaulted at the twentieth-century circus. I was in pessimistic enough humor to regret the single ring, the antique japes of a solitary clown, and the bewitching horsemanship of Mlle. Léonie, with her gauze skirts and perpetual rictus. As a matter of fact, we wouldn't endure for five minutes the old-fashioned circus and its tepid lemonade. Where are the mullygrubs of yesteryear? But the human heart is perverse. It always longs for the penny and the cake in company, while ineluctable destiny ever separates them. Perhaps my editor was right. Render unto Chopin the things that are Chopin's; send Ibsen back to his Land of the Midnight Whiskers. Smell the sawdust at the Garden, not forgetting that the chilly, dry days are at hand when even Panem et Circenses shall be taboo; when pipe and prog and grog will be banned; when these United States shall have been renamed Puritania; when a fanatically selfish minority shall take all the joy from life. Ergo, carpe diem! I thank you.

ART AND ALCOHOL

WHAT will be the reactions among artistic men and women summarily deprived of wine and malt beverages? I asked this of Manager Gatti-Casazza the other day at the Metropolitan Opera House. He is not a drinking man, but the contemptuous shrug of his shoulders showed me his position in the thrice-vexed controversy. Singers, one and all, are accustomed to mild alcoholic refreshment. If they go beyond bounds the effect on their voices is soon made manifest, but usually being foreign-born, they have been in the habit of drinking light wines at meal time, perhaps beer after a performance, for good beer relaxes nerve-tension. People don't drink beer to become intoxicated; they drink it because it lets down the pressure of a day's work better than whiskey or wine. Beer is not an intoxicant; it is a depressant. The cry that "the workingman must have his beer" is far too exclusive. The professional man, the brain-worker, needs beer, and the singer or musician — sometimes singers are not musicians! — after a nerve-exhausting performance finds in wine or beer a veritable solace. Matthew Arnold wrote that the American funny man was a national calamity. What would he have said to the plans of certain misguided females to

found "recreation centres" where, after eight
hours' exhausting daily grind, the workman
could listen to "instructive reading" — ye gods!
— and drink non-alcoholic beverages (super-
taxed?). Little wonder Bolshevism is growing
apace in an America that soon will be a vast
Dry Tortugas.

In one of her always interesting novels Ger-
trude Atherton depicts a poet whose inspiration
dried up when he stopped drinking. Swinburne
is said to have been Mrs. Atherton's model;
when the English poet ceased his cognac his
muse did not fly far afterward. If he had not
become temperate in regard to spirituous liquors
the greatest Victorian poet would have died.
Walter Savage Landor, and after him Byron,
wrote that brandy is a drink fit only for heroes.
The puny physique of Swinburne could ill brook
alcoholic excesses. His friend and protector,
Theodore Watts-Dunton, literally saved the
effervescent Algernon Charles from sudden
death. As a rule lyric poets need no stimulant.
Youth is the propulsive force to their lyricism.
If Byron drank heavily at times, Shelley was
ever a water-drinker. No rules can be formu-
lated. There is Bernard Shaw, the "Uncle
Gurnemanz" and venerable busybody of international politics. He is a fierce teetotaler. He
has confessed that family reasons prompted him
to become so, although Archdale Reid in Hered-
ity has shown that acquired traits are not inherited; that the children of drunkards are sel-

dom drunkards (prohibitionists declare the opposite, but figures can be made to lie). By the same token the sons of clergymen are not often pious. Nature abhors uniformity. If Shaw had taken his ale like the British workmen he harangues, he would not have been the pestiferous nuisance he is to-day. But, like all "reformers," "uplifters," and public nuisances, he has a weak stomach. Because he is virtuous! — the motto of all these Malvolios, these tailless foxes. Mind your own business! Ah! that's the true golden rule. There would be no wars if this custom prevailed.

The late Lombroso-Levi, formulator of many ingenious and amusing theories concerning the stigmata of genius, has collected some names of men who drank, nevertheless who contrived to leave the world in their debt for their art. Max Nordau followed his "master" with his absurd tome on Degeneration, and then the system, chiefly framed for imbeciles, quite collapsed. Professor William James sent the cardboard structure into thin air when he revealed its numerous inconsistencies. Any stigma applicable to genius or talent may be found in your shoemaker, butcher, or policeman, from megalomania to alcoholism, from faun-like ears with attached lobes to an unholy greed for other people's money. Let us look at Lombroso's list of alcoholic men of genius. He writes that Alexander died after having emptied ten times the goblet of Hercules (some thirst!). Julius Cæsar was often carried home on the shoulders of his friends — so was a certain highest dignitary in the United States during the last century, and a mediocrity he was. Socrates, Seneca, Alcibiades, Cato, Peter the Great, the Czarina Catherine were notorious boozers. Tiberius Nero was nicknamed Biberius Mero. Septimius Severus and Mahomet II died in delirium tremens. Jan Steen and Frans Hals were heavy imbibers. Hals, who lived to an advanced age and painted masterpieces to the last, was drunk every night. So was Monticelli, absinthe proving his ruin. George Morland drank, and Turner, too; both drank to excess. As for the poets and literary men, the litany is long. Henry Murger, Gerard de Nerval, Alfred de Musset, Kleist, Poe, Hoffmann, Addison, Steele, Carew, Sheridan, Burns, Charles Lamb, James Thomson, Hartley Coleridge, James Clarence Mangan, Ernest Dowson, Swinburne — Rossetti, who drugged — and Coleridge, De Quincey and Mme. de Staël abused opium.

In the domain of music examples are as thick as bombs were at Verdun. Handel swallowed a mighty amount of firewater, for he was a mighty man. Gluck drank far more than was good for him. It was a pleasing habit of his to have a harpsichord placed in some pretty rural spot, where, with a regiment of bottles, he played and composed. He died, so it is said, of brandy. Tasso drank, Baudelaire drugged and drank, and Lenau, poet, died from alcohol. Mozart and

Beethoven abused wine. Beethoven was often "a little how come ye so!" Modern instances multiply. Singers, players, actors, authors, composers — how many there are about whose heads is the aura of alcoholism! Alcohol has been the nursing bottle of genius, and of many commonplace citizens may not the same be said? Woe to him who abuses the priceless gift. He is doomed. And doomed, too, is the prohibitionist who overindulges in flapjacks and fried steak. Native cookery has slain more than the rum mills of the universe. And notwithstanding our vaunted cosmopolitanism, a natural outcome of the great war, the village pump is to be our national Totem. Butchered to make a prohibitionist holiday; that prohibition which has elevated "legislation" to the dignity of a sport.

Richard Wagner possessed an irritable stomach, but was comforted by a glass of good wine (as apparently was St. Paul). Walt Whitman neither smoked nor drank. Poor Guy de Maupassant began with wine, and, in the wake of erotic excesses, he resorted to opium, even to ether, which he would put on his handkerchief and apply to his nostrils. Such a hatred of reality was his! He well deserved the appellation of "Taureau triste," as he was surly toward the end of a brilliant career. Flaubert, like Zola, was chary of excess, except in literary work. Be chaste in your life that you may be violent in your art! he enjoined de Maupassant.

Turgénieff, Daudet, Huysmans, Gounod, Goncourt, were not alcoholic. Bizet, it is said, died of absinthe, not of disappointment over the failure of Carmen; which didn't fail, as Philip Hale has shown us. Goethe was wild in his youth, drank wine, pursued the golden girl, yet he cannot by any stretch of imagination be placed in the ranks of the drunkards. The alcoholic neurosis exists in the individual, who drinks because he is neurotic, and is not necessarily neurotic because he is a drunkard. As usual, the prohibitionists have put the cart before the horse, being ignorant, or pretending to be, of facts disclosed by modern biological research. These fanatics suffer from what might be called psychical dandruff.

What am I trying to prove? Nothing. Alcohol inspired or spurred on these men, and we are the inheritors of their visions. Naturally, to the boneheads who engineer reforms, all art is dangerous, is immoral. Art, like religion, is also an opiate. God made the dawn, but the devil invented the evening. The Seven Arts are the invention of men in revolt against the tedium of life. Killing time is only killing one's self, for we are crucified at the crossroads of Time and Space (with the Button-Moulder lurking around the corner). To escape the eternal ennui man created the arts, and music, the most soothing of the seven, has drugged his dreams and made fantastic the rude angles of concrete life. Perhaps music is only a majestic noise.

135

Sometimes it bruises the soul as do bells the air. It can retire majestically into the recesses of the imagination, like the faint roar of surf withdrawn on the beach of Time. It may be a ballet for triphammers or as splendidly sonorous as the color chords of Picasso or the tortured mechanisms of Marcel Duchamps. But always an opiate, a consoler.

The truth is that our existence without some buffer between our naked souls and the chill wind of empty spiritual space would be inconceivable. Man devised Time and Space — symbols of his terrifying ignorance in the presence of eternity — and religion and the arts wherewith he might cloak his nakedness. All the rest is vanity. Prohibition is only a symptom of the everlasting propensity of intolerant minds to fashion others after their own mean image. There is no need to worry over it. Like other tyrannical devices to enslave the will of mankind, it will be tested, found wanting, and dropped. And the best way to hasten the decease is to enforce rigidly the law. But come what may, art and alcohol are inseparably wedded, as in the Greek myth Apollo and Dionysos imaged beauty and ecstasy.

THE TRAGIC CHOPIN

CHOPIN has bequeathed to us six scherzos. The four that comprise a group are opus 20, in B minor; opus 31, B flat minor; opus 39, C sharp minor, and opus 54, E major. The two remaining scherzos are in the second sonata, opus 35, and in the third sonata, opus 58. They are in the respective keys of E flat minor and E flat major. These six compositions are evidences of the power, originality, variety, and delicacy of Chopin. The scherzo is formally not his invention. Beethoven and Mendelssohn anticipated him: But he remodelled the form and filled it with a surprisingly novel content, though not altering its three-four measure. With the Beethoven scherzo we realize the swing, the robustiousness and, at times, the rude jollity. In the Mendelssohn scherzo we enjoy the velocity and finish. Light without heat, true scherzando moods; indeed, more scherzo-like than Chopin's, Mendelssohn's sense of elfin joy stemmed from the early Italian masters of the pianoforte. Rossini voiced this belief after hearing the scherzo a capriccio from the nimble fingers of Felix himself, and said to the composer: "That smells of Scarlatti." And it does recall Domenico Scarlatti, whose compositions, slight as to structure, are replete with gracious vitality and a surface skimming of sentiment like the curved flight of a thin bird over shallow waters.

A terrible though beautiful domain is the Chopin scherzo. Only two have the lightness of touch, clarity in atmosphere and bustling gaiety of the conventional scherzo: the other four are fierce, grave, ironic, sardonic, fiery, passionate, even hysterical, and most melancholy. In several the moods are pathologic; in all, magical. The scherzo in E, opus 54, may be best described by the thrice commonplace word, delightful. It is sunny music, and its sweep and swiftness are compelling. The five preluding bars of half-notes, unison, strike the keynote of optimism. What follows is like the ruffling of tree-tops by warm southern winds. The little upward flight in E, beginning at the seventeenth bar, in major thirds and fourths, has been cleverly utilized by Saint-Saens in the scherzo of his G minor piano concerto, opus 22. The fanciful embroidery of the single finger passages is never opaque; a sparkling, bubbling freedom and freshness characterize this Chopin scherzo, a composition not heard too often in public, possibly because there are few pianists, like Joseffy or De Pachmann, to play it. Its emotional content is not deep; it lies well within the category of the elegant, the capricious. Its fourth page contains an episode which at first blush suggests the theme of the A flat valse, opus 42, with its comminglement of duplex and

triple rhythms. Although the piu lento is in C
sharp minor, it betrays little sadness; it is but
the blur of a passing cloud that shadows with
its fleecy edges the wind-swept moorland.

This scherzo in E is a mood of joyousness; as
joyous as the witty, sensitive, umbrageous composer ever allowed himself to become. Its coda
is not so forcible as the usual Chopin coda.
There is a dazzling flutter of silvery scale at the
close. Altogether a charming work. Closely
allied to it in general sentiment is the E flat
scherzo from the B minor sonata. It is largely
arabesque and its ornamentation is genial
though not surprisingly ingenious. It somewhat savors of Weber. It might go on forever.
The resolution is not intellectual; it is purely
one of tonality. The thought is tenuous. But
it is highly embroidered relief after the first
movement of the sonata. Nor is the trio in B
particularly noteworthy. Truly a salon scherzo,
which challenges Mendelssohn on his native
heath. It may be considered as an intermezzo,
also as a prelude to the lyric measures.

We are on firm and familiar footing when the
first page is opened of the B flat minor scherzo,
the second in order of composition. Who has
not heard with interest those overarching and
questioning triplets which Chopin could never
make his pupils play sufficiently "tombé"? He
told De Lenz: "It must be a charnel-house."
Alas! These same vaulted phrases have since
become banal. This scherzo, like the lovely

A flat Ballade, is cruelly tortured by the ambitious musical flapper. Yet how great, how vigorous, it all is; how it abounds in sweetness and light when the music falls from the fingers of a master! It is a Byronic poem — "so tender, so bold, as full of love as of scorn," to quote Schumann. Has Chopin ever penned a more delicious song than this in D flat, with its straying over the tonal borderland? It is the high noon of life. The dark bud of the introduction has come to a perfect flowering, and with what miracles of scent, shape, and color! The second section has the quality of sane wit. It is serious to severity, yet its meanings are noble. The brief excursion that follows is the awakening from a wondering dream; no suggestion there of pallid morbidities. And how supremely welded is the style with the subject; what masterly writing evolved from the genius of the instrument! Then, fearful that he has dwelt too long upon his ideas, Chopin, in a rapturous flight, soars away to clear sky. After the repetition comes the development section, and while it is ingenious and effective in a chaotic way, nevertheless it is here that the composer is at his weakest. The Olympian aloofness of Beethoven, which permitted him to survey his material from every point of view, Chopin could not boast. He is a great composer, but he was also a great pianist. He nurses his themes with constructive frugality, and sometimes the mechanical limitation of the piano checks his imagination.

The well-sounding is considered as much as the clearly thought. There is logic in his exposition, though it is often piano, not music, logic. A certain straining after brilliancy, a falling off in the spontaneous urge of the earlier pages, force us to feel easier with the return of the first theme. The coda is brilliant. This scherzo in B flat minor bids fair to remain the favorite among its fellows. It is neither cryptic nor repellent, like the first and third scherzo. It is a perennial joy to pupil and public. Like the soliloquy in Hamlet, the B flat minor scherzo is become a popular quotation.

Its predecessor in B minor, opus 20, is the profounder of the pair, but not so melodious. It is the most shrill and hysterical of the scherzos. Though in the ironic vein, it is Chopin recklessly throwing himself to the winds of remorse — a Manfred mood, a mood of self-torture, a confession from the first chord to the last. Within the dream inclosed by its gates of tonal brass there is the struggle of an imprisoned soul. It is the unhappiest and the most riotous of the Pole's works, and it is also unduly long. Its emotional keynote is too tense to permit of the repetitions marked by the composer. These repetitions are unsuited to present taste, which, above all, demands brevity. Poignancy and prolixity are mutually exclusive. The piece greatly gains when played without "da capo." Its first part is so drastically harsh that the

succeeding melody in B, with its lilting tenths
— "the sweet slumber of the moonlight on the
hill" — after the tragic strain comes as benison.
This scherzo seems to possess a personal message. Chopin, like Robert Louis Stevenson, was
consumptive. Slender of frame, as was the
Scotch writer, his spirit was leonine. His was
psychic bravery. He could write terrible music,
conjure up desperate images. A sense of stifled
longing, of the inability to compass his lofty
ambitions, fill this first scherzo. It is the tragedy of Chopin's life compressed within a few
pages; the tragedy of one whose spirit was
weaker than his flesh.

The arabesques after the eight-bar introduction — some of them muted bars, as is Chopin's
wont — has a spiritual resemblance to the principal figure in the Fantasie-Impromptu, opus
66; but instead of the ductile triplets, as in the
bars of the Impromptu, the figure in the scherzo
is divided between the hands, while the harsh-
ness of the mood is emphasized by the anticipa-
tory chord in the left hand. The vitality of
this first page is positively electrifying. The
questioning chords at the close of the section
are as imaginative as any passage ever written
by the composer. The half-notes E and the
upleaping appogiaturia are evidences of his
originality in minor details. These occur before the modulation into the lyric theme and
with some slight dashes before the dash into the
coda. The second section, in agitato, contains

several knotty harmonic problems; they must be skimmed over at tempestuous speed, else cacophony. Here Chopin is bold to excess, as if his spirit would knock at the very gates of heaven or hell. But the thunder and surge, after waxing, soon wanes and spends itself. The soul has stormed itself into sheer weariness. By critical consent, the molto piu lento is a masterpiece. Written in the luscious key of B, it is like a woven enchantment. Chopin attains most subtle effects with broken accords in tenths. The only other slow movements comparable to this are the B major episode in the B minor octave study, opus 25, and the largo of the B minor sonata. The Garden of Armida or the Vale of Tempe are evoked by all three tone-poems.

Mark how the composer resumes his first savage mood. It is a picture of contrasted violences. Beware of the "da capo." Too many repetitions provoke satiety. Rather attack at once the coda — that most dramatic of Chopin's codas. Bold, breathless, startling, is this impetuous ride 'cross country. The heavy accentuation on the first note of every bar should not obscure one's rhythmic sense to the second beat in the left, which is likewise accented. This produces mixed rhythms, which add to the murkiness, confusion, and despair of the finale. These daring dissonances — so daring, so logical, so dramatic — how they must have rasped the nerves of Chopin's contemporaries! And they should be rigorously insisted upon. No veiled half-lights. All bridges are burned. Naught remains but catastrophe. To his doom goes this musical Childe Roland! The Dark Tower crumbles as the poet dauntlessly blows his slug-horn. The scherzo ends in overwhelming ruin. The last page is a supreme offering to the god of pessimism.

Even though the sneering fretfulness of an unhappy sick-brained man disturbs its sharp contours, the third scherzo in C sharp minor, opus 39, is the most dramatic and the finest moulded of them all. It is capricious to madness, but the dramatic quality is unmistakable. It seethes with scorn — if such an extravagant expression may be allowed; but it is extravagant, full of fire and fury, yet signifying something. A word as to the tempo: The scherzos, with a few exceptions, are marked presto, but we must remember that it is the presto of Chopin's time, also of his piano action. His favorite Pleyel piano was light and elastic in action. To-day actions are heavier, the key dip greater, though the elasticity is the same. Therefore the tempi of these scherzos — or should I write scherzi? — ought to be moderated, otherwise the music loses its significant ponderability, not to say dignity, when we adopt the old-fashioned time markings. The first part of the B minor scherzo may be taken at a presto pace — that is, a commodious presto, the scherzo in E major must be played presto; also the one in E flat, as both are of the velocity genre; but when the thought takes on a graver hue, where the mastery of utterance and nobility of phrase are to be considered, then moderate your pulse-beat. The scherzo in C sharp minor is a special sufferer from a too hurried speed. Architectonics are blurred, details jumbled and grandeur of style is absent. And if you start with such a fiery tempo, how shall you secure contrast in the coda, which should be fairly shot from the finger-tips? Or would you emulate Schumann in his G minor sonata, in the finale, which begins prestissimo, and is later ordered by the composer to become still more prestissimo? Achieve a presto, by all means, but consider the heavier tonal mass of the modern piano.

This C sharp minor scherzo is a massive composition, yet replete with fitful starts and rhythmic surprises. The chorale and its trio are Chopinesque as to fioritura and in harmonic basis. Throughout the narrative tone is dramatic; even in the "meno mosso" it never tarries. The coda is built on an effect of persistent iteration. It is excellently adapted to the keyboard. The composition has affinities with the dark and grotesque conceptions of Hoffmann, Poe, or Coleridge. Its acid irony recalls Heine. It is like fantastic architecture seen in a dream; about it hover perpetual gloom and the despairing things that circle in the night. It is like a tale from Poe's iron-bound, melancholy volume of the Magi and across its portal is written the word, Spleen.

Remains the E flat minor scherzo from the second sonata. It is the most powerful of the set. To interpret, one needs breadth of style, heroic spirit, abetted by wrists of steel. The big Rossinian one-bar crescendo at the beginning taxes the strength. The composition is elemental; the chromatic whistling of the wind in the chord of the sixth makes true storm-music. There is menacing gloom in the initial bars; the blissful song is not quite uninterrupted bliss; there is always a tempest that threatens. The descending octaves, which seem to invite us to the infernal regions, are swept away by the storm-theme, and once more we are madly projected through space. Satanic pride, a challenge to fate, the defiance of the microcosm to the threatening macrocosm; these and other characteristics may be imagined in this profound work. It depends on the listener. With Chopin as with Rome, you carry away what you fetch to either man or city. But your little Peter's pence of sympathy has suffered a rich change in the return. We are the gainers. Some day, no longer as remote as when the fallacious belief that the music of any particular nation is better than another's, perhaps Chopin may stand where he should, next to Bach, Mozart, and Beethoven. There is no such thing as map-music; there is only beautiful music. And you can never play Chopin beautifully enough.

PHASES OF THE GREATER
CHOPIN

To-day the Impromptus of Chopin are well-nigh impossible in the concert-room. Those delights of all true "flappers," the Fantasie-Impromptu in C sharp minor, and the A flat Impromptu are played too often, that is, played badly. The first part of the Fantasie-Impromptu is taken at too swift a pace, and, in consequence, sounds too much like an etude, when in reality its arabesques do hint at something more emotional. The figuration suggests that of the B minor scherzo, not, however, so pregnant with dramatic meanings. And that second section in D flat, how it is dragged, how it is sprawled and drawled! In company with the second theme of the Funeral March, it is the most sentimental of its composer. The greater Chopin is revealed in the second Impromptu, the one in the key of F sharp major. It is a sheaf of moods organically more bound together than seems at a first hearing. Because of its true impromptu spirit, its vagrant moods, its restless outpouring of fancies, it has been rather disregarded by some Chopinists, who, hidebound as any academic critic, are shocked by the changes in tonality, and, being unimaginative, are shocked also by the capricious shifting of moods; one dream melts into another, and after a repetition of those sweetly attuned chords at the close, a vigorous affirmation awakens the listener as would a sudden clap of thunder during a peaceful evening in June. There are several enigmatic bars of modulation that have puzzled purists and still are disquieting even to excursionists through the tangled harmonic underwoods of Ornstein and Stravinsky. I refer to a transitional passage after the march-like measures and immediately before the return of the principal melody. Elsewhere I have compared them to the creaking of a rusty hinge in the dooryard where Walt Whitman's lilacs last bloomed. The G flat Impromptu, the third in the published order — the Fantasie-Impromptu, opus 66, is posthumous — was seldom heard in recital till Vladimir de Pachmann, master expositor of the more delicate phases of the Polish composer, revived it in his programme. Since then it is become more familiar. It is charming with its spiral figuration, though less novel than its two predecessors.

The Mazurkas, those impish, morbid, gay, sour, dour, graceful little dances, I need not dwell upon here at length. For the majority of pianists they are a sealed book, and if you have not a savor of Slav in you pray do not disturb them with your literalism. De Pachmann, Godowsky, Paderewski, Gabrilowitsch, and Josef Hofmann play them wonderfully, but how few others. I recall a story told me by Rosenthal, whose colossal performances here are memorable. He wished to hear from De Pachmann's nimble fingers his own version of the Mazurkas and paid the Russian a visit one evening. Pachmann did not greet Rosenthal too sympathetically. "Ah!" he exclaimed, when Moriz, the octave-thunderbolt, explained the reason for his unexpected appearance. "Ah! but I play the Mazurkas so badly. Now, if I had your technique"— his eyes fairly sparkled with malicious irony —"I might be able to play them!" However, he was persuaded, and once seated at the piano he didn't leave it till he had almost finished the entire collection; and Chopin wrote many of these dances. (At least fifty-one, if you include several of doubtful authenticity). How did he play them, this perverse magical artist? Rosenthal told me that he had never heard such beautiful, subtle, and treacherous playing; the treachery was the manner in which he interpreted the music. Not an accent was correct, the phrasing was falsified, though the precise notation was adhered to, and all delivered with a variety of touches positively exquisite. "There!" cried De Pachmann, as he finished, "that is the only way to play the Mazurkas." And he smiled with his eyes. "Not!" thought Rosenthal, who thanked his colleague and hurried into the open air where he could explode. Talk about camouflage! The joke was later when Rosenthal teased De Pachmann about his trickery and the Chopinzee absolutely grinned with joy. Surely, as Sam Johnson remarked, the reciprocal civility of authors is one of the most risible scenes in the farce of life. The splenetic doctor could have joined musicians to authors.

Chopin has composed some marvellous music in the Mazurka form. Consider the three or four of these dances in the key of C sharp minor, the poetic one in B flat minor, the one with the morbidly insistent theme in B minor or that sad, appealing example in F minor, the last which Chopin is said to have put on paper. Its fixed idea, its hectic gaiety and acrid gloom reveal a sick brain, the brain of a dying man. But there are many other Mazurkas filled with daylight cheerfulness. Of the greater Chopin posterity will probably acclaim the Polonaises in F sharp minor, A flat major and the Fantaisie-Polonaise in the same key. There is a wealth of fantasy in this Polonaise, opus 61; its restless tonalities, the beauty of the first theme, the vaporous deliquesence later of this theme, the violent mood changes and harmonic grandeur left this work to the elect of the composer. The F sharp minor Polonaise and the so-called Siberian in E flat minor, as well as the Polonaise in C minor are nothing if not virile. They demand men as well as pianists to interpret them.

PHASES OF THE GREATER CHOPIN

Liszt pronounced the F sharp minor Polonaise pathologic. As a matter of fact, it surpasses in sombre grandeur the Heroic Polonaise, opus 53, notwithstanding the thundering cannons and cavalry charges of the more popular of the pair. The triplets in eight notes of the introduction achieve a splendid climax of suspense before the entrance of the chief theme. Soon octaves and chords supplant the single notes of the melody. There is epical breadth which at each reiteration becomes bigger, so big that it almost overflows the frame of the keyboard, in suggestion becomes orchestral. The second subject in the major (D flat) is less drastic, is an excellent contrast figure. The strange intermezzo in A which precedes the Mazurka is not enigmatic if you hear it as a sinister roll of drums. I think of Rembrandt's Night Watch, and its muffled morning music. Its intent is manifest, it leads to the second theme, now transposed to the despairing key of C sharp minor; the Mazurka which follows tempted Liszt — or his amanuensis, Princess Sayn-Wittgenstein — to the most extravagant panegyric. Its brace of double notes, thirds and sixths are lovely in hue and scent, but pray do not languish your tempo, else the episode soon becomes sugary. Again the Polonaise resumes its elemental chant, a chant which grows huger in rancorous woe until the very bottom of the pit of desolation is reached, and, without a gleam of light, comes the code with mutterings of the main theme, and only in the very last bar we hear with positive relief a smashing F sharp in octaves.

What does it all mean? Some obscure psychological drama of the composer's soul in which he vents his spleen, indignation and defiance, and rages against the ineluctable canons of destiny. In a sense this Polonaise is pathologic. It appeals to the nerves. It lacerates the pulp of our sensibility, it is morbid, but it is also magnificent. It is not sensational like the two Polonaises of Liszt in E major and C minor, though it is equally brilliant. Arthur Friedheim played the Chopin Polonaise superbly at one time. It suited his saturnine mood. I fancy, however, that Franz Liszt's performance must have been the supreme exemplar. There is a loftiness of mood coupled with the heroic patterns of this piece which place it in the category of masterpieces. It reminds one of a sullen, rugged landscape in the style of Salvator Rosa, a solitary human in the foreground, distracted, who lifts suicidal hands to the darkling, indifferent skies. It is the tragedy of Man, who is no longer, as in the old-fashioned geocentric conception of the universe, the centre of things, but discovers himself alone, deserted by the familiar signs and stars in his cosey firmament, and despairs. The tragedy of unfaith. The tragedy of love that slays. Unhappy Chopin was baptized a Roman Catholic, so was George Sand. Both were, to put the case mildly, slack in the practices of their church. Chopin was of a pious bent.

He concealed his attachment to the French sphinx of the inkpot from his mother in Warsaw because he feared to pain her. She was profoundly religious. Madame Sand, who didn't wear trousers and smoke all day, as caricature proclaims, was cruel to her consumptive genius. She appreciated his work, but his humors were antic. She called Frederic "mon cher cadavre," and this "corpse" must have grated on his nerves. Oh! if he had possessed but a tithe of her saving sense of humor. But Chopin was not given to jesting over his love. He flirted and mildly diverted himself; the Sand affair was deadly serious to him. When the spirit moved her she betrayed him (let us politely call it spirit rather than temperament). Her final desertion didn't kill him. It was the liaison that slew the man, body and soul. She robbed him of love, faith, and fatherland. His ending, though, was in the proper religious key. According to Turgines, half the countesses in Europe sang him to his death. (Many are still singing their hearers along the same road.) I believe the F sharp Polonaise to be the most subjective from the pen of its composer, even more so than the B minor scherzo, opus 20.

The nocturnes are done to death. Let us pass them by. The C sharp minor nocturne is like the one in C minor; both are still free from persecution at the hands of the young person who has decked the most virile spirit of his age with Parisian millinery. These two nocturnes do not intrigue the fancy of the amateur. In breadth of conception they are Beethovenian. The E major nocturne, a favorite of Josef Hofmann, and the one in B, the Tuberose, in which Paderewski proved so eloquent and whose very title makes H. L. Mencken grit his teeth, are loaded with purest Chopin ore. I admire, but with reservations, the transcription of various nocturnes to instruments of the string family. Wilhelmj transposed the D flat nocturne for violin and Leopold Auer has arranged the posthumous nocturne in E minor, which Heifetz plays beautifully; yet, effective as they may be, they are not truly Chopinesque. They are too saccharine on the strings; we miss the cool, crystalline tones of the pianoforte.

The Berceuse! Of that wonder-child who came to us through the pink gates of the dawn, and was rocked to rhythmic dreams in Chopin's Cradle Song, I may only say that in the hands of many pianists it has grown to be a brat of banal visage and muscular proportions. An ululation of the D flat tonality, it has now become a mere finger study. When Joseffy played the composition a poem emerged from the ivories. What of the Preludes? Alone the twenty-five Preludes would give their creator a claim on immortality. There are technical range and poetic vision; above all, there is humanity. Shades of feeling are explored, depths and altitudes of passion explored. If all Chopin were to be annulled I should plead for the salvation of the Preludes. The cameo-like stillness of some is like softly spoken words overheard in a cloister. Truly religious. But thunder-riven Preludes in D minor, in B flat minor, in F minor and E flat minor stir our pulse to sharper vibration. Surpassingly sweet is the elegiac Prelude in B flat. It recalls the nocturnes. The second Prelude with its enig-matic questionings is for a rainy day; a day when the soul is racked by doubt or defeat; about it, hovers a grisly something that we dare not define. It may be Chopin's Horla, this sinister music-making. A ray of sunshine, but from a sun that slants in the west is the Prelude in G. What marvels in miniature, what cun-ningly wrought jewels! Darker drama may be found as the D minor Prelude with its ele-mental ground — bass — in angry sea roars somewhere in the background; also in the glit-tering scales of the B flat minor Prelude and the declamatory passages of the F minor Pre-lude. In the C sharp minor Prelude, opus 45, there are marked anticipations of the later manner of Brahms, not alone in spirit but in figuration. This Prelude is a foretaste of Brahms, the familiar Chopin note not missing.

The embroideries of the Barcarolle — a fully developed and dramatic Nocturne — and of the Bolero are more Polish than Italian or

Spanish. By some critics the Fantaisie, opus 49, has been adjudged the most perfect work of the composer. The grave, march-like introductions, the insistent, climbing figures in triplets, the great song in F minor, followed by the enchanting episodes in double-notes, and the powerful climax reveal another Chopin from the sentimental dreamer, the conventional Thaddeus of Warsaw. There is logical development. There are dramatic scope and intensity. The lento is peaceful, the coda impressive. The entire composition is massive, its phraseology long-breathed. It represents the master at the peak of his powers.

THE TWILIGHT OF COSIMA I

WHEN Cosima I, Queen of Baireuth, does enter the eternal shadowland, her passing will not greatly intrigue the attention of a world whose ears buzz with the rumors of mightier happenings. She has been a dweller for years in the Twilights. (She was born December 25, 1837, at Bellagio, Italy, and not in 1840, as the musical annals have it.) She is the last of the famous dynasty founded by her husband, Richard Wagner, greatest of modern composers. No one, not even his admirers, dared pretend that Siegfried Wagner would ever succeed his father on the musical throne. A brief span Cosima entertained high hopes for her son's future. He had been coached by Humperdinck and Richter. His operas were produced in European capitals, but to no avail. He could not fill the shadow of his sire, much less write a bar of music worth the whistling. Wotan had fathered a Parsifal, Jr., and Baireuth sympathized with Cosima's disappointment. It was the second sorrow of a life crowded with happiness. In 1883 the man she adored as a god died on her bosom at Venice. That tragic event transformed her from a loving wife to the sternly ambitious woman who ruled the destinies of Baireuth for thirty years. In 1913 the third sorrow came to her in the unwelcome shape of copyright expiration. The music of Wagner was free to every country. Parsifal, the Rhinegold of Baireuth, already had been ravished by an American Alberich; nevertheless, from the shock of the legal decision which blotted Baireuth off the map of music Cosima never recovered. She was become a shadow of her former grandeur. She had outlived her majesty.

I first saw her in 1894. It was the summer when Lillian Nordica made her début in the historic opera-house on the hill. Zoltan Doeme, her husband, also appeared. His Parsifal, too, is historic. Queen Cosima I was a tall, gaunt woman with the familiar Liszt profile, her white hair worn à la Liszt, her stride that of a grenadier. She ruled with an iron hand, a hand not encased in a velvet glove like her father's. A tyrant in petticoats was the usual ascription. Not loved, indeed feared, she ran the Baireuth machine with the shrewdness of a Tammany Hall politician. Her contemporaries concur in that. A woman of brains, courage, audacity, she recalled for me a second Margravine of Baireuth in her domineering manner. She would tolerate no rivals. Conductor after conductor came and went. When Lilli Lehmann toward the close of a glorious artistic career sang, in 1896, then Gibraltar met Gibraltar. Lilli had been one of the Rhine-Daughters in 1876. She knew her Wagner as well as Cosima. There was warlike gossip then of which I got my fill. The ladies parted the best of friends, of course. Olive Fremstad, a pupil of Lehmann, was one of the Rhine-Daughters that year. Ellen Gulbranson was the Brünnhilde after Lehmann. Alois Burgstaller made a clumsy début as Siegfried and Parsifal. Mottl was the reigning favorite, Felix of Munich, the first man in whom the inconsolable Cosima showed deep interest after the death of Richard. Cosima, all said and done, was a daughter of Franz Liszt. The last time I saw her was in 1901. With George Moore I stood on the esplanade facing the Franconian valley, and during an entr'acte of the Ring we discussed the mediocre conducting of Prince Siegfried Wagner and the fond, foolish affection of his mother. She passed. This time she rode, but that rigid spine, the proud pose of the head, the undimmed hawk-like eyes — I am the widow of Wagner and the daughter of Liszt! they seemed thus to challenge the gaze of the public — proved her still in possession of all her powers. And she was then past sixty. Truly an extraordinary woman this, with her name out of the Italian Renaissance, herself like some belated and imperious apparition from the Renaissance.

Her forebears were just as remarkable. Liszt met her mother, the Countess d'Agoult, in the brilliant whirl of his artistic successes at Paris. Chopin had dedicated to her the first book of his Études. She was beautiful, accomplished, though her intimates declare that hers was not a truthful nature. She was born Marie Sophie de Flavigny, in 1805, at Frankfort-on-Main, Germany. Her father was the Vicomte de Flavigny, a French refugee, who had married the daughter of Simon Moritz Bethmann, a rich banker, originally from Amsterdam and a Hebrew converted to Lutheranism. Marie had literary ability, boasted of meeting Goethe once, and in 1827 she married Count Charles d'Agoult of Paris. Social sedition was in the air. The "Misunderstood Woman" — no new thing then, and still with us — was the fashion. George Sand was changing her lovers with every book she wrote, and the Countess d'Agoult began to yearn for fame and adventures. Liszt appeared. He seems to have been the pursued one. They eloped. In honor he could not desert the woman. They made Geneva their home — temporarily, for both had the nomad heart and were doomed to pitch their tents in many strange places. In her own right Marie had twenty thousand francs yearly income. It cost Liszt exactly three hundred thousand francs to keep up an establishment such as the lady had been accustomed to; he earned this at the keyboard, a tidy amount for those days. (There were pianistic money-kings before Paderewski.) And yet she was not satisfied. Ever insatiable are artistic women.

Mme. d'Agoult bore him three children — Blandine, Cosima, and Daniel. Blandine, the beauty of the family, married Emile Ollivier in

1857. She died in 1862. Liszt greatly loved her. Ollivier was later Napoleon's war minister, and was fooled to the top of his bent by the Mephisto of European politics, Count von Bismarck. He died a few years ago nearly a centenarian, and busy to the last explaining that he was not to blame for losing the tragic Franco-Prussian War. His hell was paved with good intentions before he reached there. Cosima married Hans von Bülow, her father's "favorite pupil" (there were hundreds of them), in 1857. True to family form, she ran off with Richard Wagner, and, to the despair of her father, married that fickle gentleman. Her father's discomfiture was the result of Cosima's defection from the Roman Catholic faith. She renounced this faith and became of her husband's religious persuasion, *i. e.*, nominally a Protestant, in reality a free-thinker. Daniel Liszt, the hope of his father, died in December, 1859, at the age of twenty. Liszt had legitimatized the birth of his children, had educated them, had generously dowered his daughters, and all three were a source of sorrow to him. The high light of comedy was not absent when the gallant Count d'Agoult — we shan't say "bereaved of his wife," for who shall pretend to analyze the mixed emotions of a man sorely wounded in his pride of race and secretly overjoyed at being rid of a pernicious blue-stocking? — called a family council, which, after due consideration, pronounced the verdict that Mon-

sieur François Liszt (they spelled it Litz in
Paris) had behaved like a "perfect gentleman"
in a certain delicate indiscretion, thereby ab-
solving him from all blame in the matter. Re-
cording angels on high must have wept, and
George Meredith lost a theme peculiarly fitted
to his ironic pen. But the injured husband
calmly went to his club every day and died in
the odor of mundane sanctity.

As might have been foreseen, la d'Agoult
quarrelled with her Liszt. They parted bad
friends. Under the pen-name of Daniel Stern
she attacked him in her souvenirs and novels.
He forgave. A most irritating trait in his character was his inability to hate his enemies. Of
Heine alone he spoke ill. When some one asked
him if Heine's name would be carved on the
portals of fame, Liszt replied: "Yes, in letters
of mud"; which is manifestly unjust. In 1860
Franz and Marie met for the last time, and in
Paris. He gently told her that the true title of
her souvenirs should have been Poses et Men-
songes. She wept. He was quite right. She
was a detestable poseuse and a fibber. Tragic
comedians, both. They bored each other.
Their union recalls Flaubert's profound remark
that Emma Bovary found in adultery only the
platitudes of marriage. Perhaps other ladies
had supervened in the cometary existence of
Liszt. Like Byron he was the sentimental hero
of his day. A René of the pianoforte. Read
the recollections of Mme. Adam for a clue to the

character of Cosima's mother. Liszt sensibly intrusted to the care of his own mother the education of her three grandchildren. She was born at Krems, Lower Austria, and a pious soul. Curious it is that the son of a Hungarian magnate's overseer should be by the force of circumstances and his own genius allied with the aristocracy and high diplomacy in several lands of his time, Liszt Ferencz, whose name translated into English would be Frank Flour.

Unhappy with the intellectual but irascible von Bülow, Cosima was happy with her Richard. If there were quarrels they were fought behind closed doors. She was not beautiful like her sister Blandine, but she had more brains. Anton Rubinstein loved her; Nietzsche's last recorded writing before his mental eclipse at Turin, 1889, was a passionate phrase meant for her. He was closely allied with the Wagners at Triebschen, and had corrected the proofs of Richard's Autobiography, a garbled version of which has been published with the blue pencil of Baireuth writ large on every page. Some day all the secrets of that prison-house will be divulged. Nietzsche surmised much, and many guesses have furnished stuff for romantic commentators. Romance of the most lurid pattern has enveloped the Liszt Wagner von Bülow d'Agoult group. And the greatest influence in Wagner's career was not Cosima but Mathilde Wesendonck, to whom we owe the genesis of that lyric masterpiece among masterpieces, Tristan and Isolde.

For her spiritual collaboration with Wagner, Mathilde was never forgiven by Cosima — after all, a real woman.

Liszt participated in the musical inauguration of Baireuth, in 1876; the family dissension had been patched up in 1873; but he played second fiddle to his son-in-law. His affectionate daughter saw to that; also saw, in 1886, when her father had the bad taste to die during the festival at Baireuth, that he was buried as quietly as possible, for an imposing funeral might have disturbed the gate-money at the big barn on the hill. Thrift, Cosima, thrift! At her husband's death she declared that her father no longer existed for her. Mention of his music was snubbed at Wahnfried — in the back yard of which Wagner was buried like a cat, as Philip Hale so blandly puts it. The awful part was to follow. Liszt, instead of being interred at Weimar, or Budapest, lies under the shelter of a hideous tomb in Baireuth, devised by his grandson, Siegfried Wagner — who is also an architect. This, another of Cosima's tactless doings. She estranged the old friends of her husband, with the exception of the faithful Hans Richter, who told me at London — in 1901, where he conducted the Ring in Covent Garden — that Cosima was as great as a woman as Wagner a composer; which was no doubt true; and she was also a meddlesome blunderer. She put Baireuth on the map of Cook's Trippers. She botched artistically every performance she handled, but she made money; her banker-grandfather's business ability she must have inherited. There is no doubt the tragedy of Germany added to her sorrows. With her will pass forever the once powerful Wagnerian dynasty.

IDLE SPECULATIONS

IF it had been hinted a half century ago that in the veins of Richard Wagner there flowed Semitic blood, laughter would have ensued. The race that Wagner reviled in speech and pamphlet — though he never disdained its generosity — the hated Jew, daring to claim kinship with him might have set in motion the spleen of the German master. Wagner's hatred of the chosen race is historical. "Das Judenthum in der Musik," is not the only expression of this contempt and dislike on the part of the man who was born in a Ghetto at Leipzig. Benefits forgotten, he seldom missed a chance to gibe at Meyerbeer or Mendelssohn or to flout some Hebrew banker who was imprudent enough to advance him funds. The Wagnerian pedigree has been subjected to critical microscopes. Bournot, who was patronized by Baireuth, wrote concerning Ludwig Geyer, the true father of the composer, that his family had been Lutheran since 1700. Which proves nothing; race, not nationality, nor yet religion, counts. Geyer, from whom Richard inherited his versatile aptitudes, was markedly Jewish in features and temperament. So was Wagner. Of the putative father, a Police Magistrate, we know little. In his autobiography Wagner avoids the subject.

But Wagner's mother, born Johanna Bertz, reveals in her portraits marked characteristics of the Jewish race. There is mystery concerning her origin; even the name of Bertz was only discovered a few years ago. Bertz, too, like Geyer, is a Jewish name. There is in the polemical writings of Richard an almost insane hatred of the Jew; and, ironic circumstance, in his music there are the sensuous glow and glitter of the Oriental. It is certainly unlike any music made by a German, with its vibratile rhythms, its dramatic characterization and magnificent decorative frame. "Was Wagner German at all?" demands Nietzsche. "We have some reasons for asking this. It is difficult to discern in him any German trait whatsoever. Being a great learner, he has learned to imitate much that is German. His character itself is in opposition to what has hitherto been regarded as German — not to speak of the German musician. His father was a stage player named Geyer. A Geyer is almost an Adler — Geyer and Adler are both names of Jewish families [Vulture and Eagle, in English]. What has hitherto been put into circulation as the 'Life' of Wagner is a fable. I confess my distrust of every point which solely rests on the testimony of Wagner himself. He had not pride for any truth about himself; nobody was less proud. He remained, like Victor Hugo, true to himself in biographical matters — he remained a stage player."

Thus Nietzsche, who knew whereof he spoke, as he was the secretary of the composer at Trieb-schen when Richard dictated his autobiography; not an official secretary, but a dear friend and confidant. But Nietzsche must be taken with reservations in the Wagner case. He alter-nately adored and abused his idol. Another of his favorite contentions was that Schopenhauer ruined Wagner's art. The truth is that in Wag-ner the artist was stronger than Wagner the philosopher. The reflective man was usually overcome by the man poetic. Witness Tristan and Isolde, composed, as Richard confessed, in direct opposition, nay, defiance, of his life's theories. Wagner began with Feuerbach and ended a victim to the fascinating black magic of Schopenhauer. But now we know, thanks to James Sully's magisterial work Pessimism, that pessimism and optimism are a question of personal temperament. Wagner succumbed at the last to the Buddhistic quietism of the Scho-penhauerian theories, though his elastic, op-timistic nature rebelled at the yoke. In the Ring the pessimism never crowds out the vital dramatic power. In Parsifal the vigorous af-firmations of the earlier Wagner are absent. He said Nay to the life that had exhausted him, and, bathed in a mystic atmosphere, his soul found consolation in the mere contempla-tion of Roman Catholic symbolism.

Nevertheless, hold firmly in your mind that Richard Wagner the artist was greater than

Wagner the vegetarian, the anti-vivisectionist,
Socialist, revolutionist, Jew-hater, and foe of
Meyerbeer and Mendelssohn, also greater than
Wagner the philosopher and poet-dramatist.
He was first and last the musician. For that
reason he did not say the last word in the music-
drama. It is a mistaken partisanship that at-
taches to his every utterance profound significance. We should gladly exchange his collected prose writings for another Tristan. He
dearly loved a paradox. A versatile man, he
wore many masks. Not that we doubt his
sincerity, but that his emotional nature, his
craving for excitement, his agitated life often
led him to speak and write in misleading terms.
He seldom put his best foot foremost when he
took up the pen. And the Jews he reviled always proved his best friends.

We have often wondered where Wagner's
religion, metaphysics, his working theory of
life, would have led him had he lasted a few
years longer. That in his extraordinary brain
there had been dimly floating the outlines of a
greater work than Parsifal we learn from his
correspondence with Franz Liszt. He died with
the projected Trilogy incomplete. Tristan and
Isolde, Parsifal and the Penitent (Die Büsser)
were to have composed this Trilogy of the Will-
to-Live, Compassion and Renunciation. That
negation of the Will-to-Live, so despised by
Nietzsche, had gripped him after he became
acquainted with Schopenhauer's theories in

169

1854. He eagerly absorbed this Neo-Buddhism
and at the time of his death he was fully prepared to accept its final word, its bonze-like
impassivity of the will. In Parsifal he sought
to transpose to tone its hopelessly fatalistic
spirit, its implacable hatred of life in the flesh.
That the world has lost a gigantic experiment
may be true, but that it has lost the best of
Wagner we doubt. In Parsifal his thematic
invention is seldom at high-water mark, notwithstanding his mastery of technical material,
his marvellous moulding of spiritual stuff. Parsifal is an abstraction, while Kundry is a "howling
hermaphrodite," as Hanslick tastefully called
the poor hunted hind and harlot. It is with
Wagner's power of characterization that we
might concern ourselves, as the composer had
drifted into a philosophical nihilism — that intellectual quietism which is a treacherous pitfall
for the thinker who strays across the border-
line of Asiatic religions. The Christianity in
Parsifal seems like the last expiring glimmer of
its values. He deftly drew upon the ritual of
the Roman Catholic Church, yet in the essential Christianity of the result we place no faith.

He went to the Buddhistic roots of Christianity, perhaps for philosophical reasons. However, Nietzsche's attack on Wagner's supposed
religious predilections is wide of the mark; no
one was less likely to indulge in sacerdotal sentimentalism than the musician. The fact is
that all was grist that came to his theatrical

mill. Despite his mysticism he never lost view of the box-office. After the rude knocks of his early career he, like Balzac, realized that money is the Archimedes-lever that lifts the modern world. Money is the leading motive of the Human Comedy, and money it is that is the ruling idea of the Ring. The speculation is attractive. He changed the title of his Trilogy from The Victors (Die Sieger) to The Penitents. First considered in 1856, the name was altered a quarter of a century later. In the interval Oriental philosophy had supervened with its accustomed effect.

It was a critic of acuity who said of Tristan and Isolde that "the thrills relieve each other in squads." Wagner touched the top-notch of his torrid imaginings in this apotheosis of lyric ecstasy. Nothing has been written comparable with its intensity; its double, it is safe to predict, will never be composed. He declared that when he wrote the music he could not have made it otherwise. It is full-blown in its imperfections, glaring excellences, noble turgidity, lack of frugality, economy of thematic resources, dazzling prodigality, soggy prolixity, riotous tonal debaucheries and almost superhuman enchantments. What boots it to gird against a demoniacal art that thrills and makes mock of theories concerning the divine in music? We are no longer on the windblown heights with Beethoven, nor do we worship as in the vast Cathedral of Bach. The Schopenhauerian

philosophy hurled at us in the pessimistic dual-
ism of the love episode avails not to stem the
turbulent current of fashion. Tristan and Isolde
is the very deification of carnalism. Call it
what pretty titles you may, wreathe the theme
with poetic garlands, yet the stark fact stares
at you: The man's desire for the woman and
the woman's desire for the desire of the man,
to put the case in Biblical phraseology. The
love potion does but unloosen their tongues;
both were mute lovers before Brangaene juggled
with the fatal brew. Wagner was the greatest
poet of passion — odious, misused term — in
the history of the Seven Arts. And he had a
more potent instrument than words at his command, an orchestra that wooes and thunders,
that achieves in the surging undertow the very
soul of love. A mighty master, but a dangerous
guide is this same Richard Wagner.

THE MASTER BUILDER

THUS far this season we have heard the Third
Symphony of Brahms three times, and once the
Symphony in D, the second. These various
performances were respectively given at concerts by the Symphony Society, the Philharmonic Society, and the Philadelphia Orchestra.
Nor were they unusual happenings. The symphonic works of Brahms are perennial favorites
in New York. There is a sufficing reason.
Brahms is a transitional bridge between the
mighty Beethoven and the modern men. He
is the last of the classicists, though not precisely
the first of the romantics. Schumann was that,
not Berlioz. But Brahms is more romantic
than is commonly realized. It always will be
a mystery to the present generation why he was
called a pedant, a dry-as-dust composer. He
has his dull moments, when philosopher-like he
contemplates the umbilicus of the universe. He
is not dramatic when drama is not demanded
by his theme, and he is occasionally drab in
orchestral color, though never brilliant in the
meretricious sense. He is on the side of the
angels. He stands for what is sound, lofty,
beautiful as opposed to shallow operatic trivi-
alities and melodramatic effects.

VARIATIONS

It was unfortunate that almost at the outset of his career Edouard Hanslick, erudite, witty, malignant, should have posed Brahms as an antithetical man of straw to Richard Wagner. Doubtless it was a tempting contrast to make: Brahms, the serious symphonist, a reverent follower in the broad pathway of Bach and Beethoven; and Wagner, creator of the music-drama, of marvellous stage pictures — romantic, erotic Wagner. Yet what a fallacy is there. Brahms, as his songs, symphonies, piano, and violin music prove, was a poetic, a romantic, musician. He could not paint as boldly as Berlioz, but he always had something vital to say, while Berlioz, despite his grandiloquent rhetoric, like Victor Hugo, displayed more manner than matter. As for Wagner — well, he, too, absorbed as much of Bach and Beethoven as he could assimilate for his particular usage, and was quite as learned as Brahms. Von Bülow had set the pace for Dr. Hanslick and that detractor of Berlioz, Liszt, and Wagner, indeed of all the New Music — whenever he saw a head pop up on the horizon he hit it, like the game of Aunt Sally — recognized his opportunity and promptly pitted Brahms against Wagner, with the result that for a long period the musical world labored under the mistaken notion that Brahms was a rusty, musty old pedagogue, with bewhiskered counterpoint and a plentiful lack of melodic invention. And he was just the reverse.

He died over two decades ago and his vogue
has waxed with the years. When we consider
the list of his achievements we are amazed at
the slow, patient, yet fertile and versatile qualities of the man. "Their impatience," wrote
John Henry, Cardinal Newman, in condemning
the major defect of heresiarchs. Brahms was
ever patient. Patience might serve as his epitaph. His was a genius that grew from accre-
tions. His first opus was far from the later
Brahms, notwithstanding its potential powers.
It was but the acorn which became the great
oak of the four symphonies, the piano and the
violin concertos, the songs, chamber music,
choral compositions, the Songs of Destiny and
the Requiem. This massed work is the sum
total of a high ideal; stern, unyielding, betimes
frostily inhuman, yet logical and consistent.
The philosophic bent of his intellect extorts our
admiration. For a half century he pursued the
beautiful in its most difficult and elusive form,
followed it when the fashions of the season
mocked at such undeviating devotion, when
musical structure was called old-fashioned, sober
thought voted down as dull, when the theatre
had invaded the tonal realm and menaced it in
its very stronghold, the symphony. After all,
there is something to be said in favor of the
skeleton, whether concealed by human flesh or
embodied in religious dogma or encased within
the formal walls of musical compositions.
Things must have structure to interest mankind;

even the prudish oyster has a shell. Otherwise the amorphous shreds of the floating jellyfish or the primeval amœbæ would become our ideal. Brahms was homo sapiens. He stood on his hind legs, as did our common forebears, with "probably arboreal habits." And he wrought the noblest music since Beethoven.

He is the first composer since Beethoven to sound the note of the sublime. Naturally, Wagner is excepted because he did not write absolute music, and we are now dealing only with that form. Because of this trait of sublimity Brahms has been called austere. His austerity and lack of personal profile — sometimes — have made his loftiest music difficult of comprehension. He never splits the ears of the groundlings. He never makes any concessions to popularity. Like Ibsen and Manet, he goes out of his way to displease. The facile triumph he despises. He saw musical Europe filled with second and third rate men, and he noted that their sole excuse was to give cheap pleasure to the tasteless. This professional parasitism he abhorred; with him the reaction became a species of puritanism. It is a gratifying proof of his flexible mental operations that he understood and admired Wagner, whose ideals and practice were the antipodes of his own. His workmanship is well-nigh impeccable; formal and contrapuntal mastery marks it. His contribution to the techniques of rhythm is considerable. He literally popularized the cross-relation, rediscovered the arpeggio and elevated it to an integer of the melodic phrase. Wagner did the same for the essential turn.

His trait of fidelity, his spiritual obstinacy, are characteristic. There seems to be a notion because Brahms refused to swim the current tendencies that he held himself aloof from humanity, a bonze, a Brahmin, and not, as he really was, a bard chanting its woes and full-blooded aspirations. It is platitudinous nowadays to say that his music throbs with the rich, red blood of humanity. He is the greatest contrapuntalist since Bach (pace Richard Strauss and Max Reger), and the supreme architectonist since Beethoven. Nevertheless, in his songs he is as simple and virile as Robert Burns. His topmost peaks are remote and gleam in an atmosphere too rarefied for dwellers on the plains, but how intimate, how gracious are the happy moments in his chamber-music. Following the romantic side of Schumann, untouched by the fever of the footlights, a realist with imagination, both a classicist and a romanticist, he conducted music to its normal channel by showing that a formal service and a mastery of polyphony are not incompatible with the utterance of new ideas in a new way. Brahms is not reactionary any more than is Wagner. Neither found what he needed in contemporary life and art, so one harked back to the Greeks and Gluck, the other to Beethoven. All progress is crabwise. In the past of the arts may be found the germs of their future.

Study the massiveness of the Brahmsian tonal

architecture; study those tonal edifices erected after years of toil, consider his fertility in invention, his patience in developing his ideas; consider the ease with which he moves, though seemingly shackled by the most exacting of forms, a form not assumed for the sake of overcoming difficulties, but because it was the only form in which he could fully express himself. The narrative-tone of the symphonic form — and this includes all its practitioners from Haydn to Tschaikovsky — is like blank verse, it has been the chosen field of the greatest masters; and who shall say that either Shakespeare or Beethoven has suffered from its adoption? Even such a Romantic, mad and morbid, as Charles Baudelaire employed as his vehicles of expression forms as restricted and rigid as the sonnet and the alexandrine. Note the leaven of genius which militates against pedantry, scholastic aridity, academic music-making, and music arithmetical. Consider the intellectual and emotional brain — for the seat of the emotions is in the head, not the heart — of this composer, and then realize that all art is the arduous victory of great minds over great imaginations. Recall the introductions to the first and last movements of the Symphony in C minor by Brahms. That magnificent work makes by comparison other men's efforts like facile improvising. Its bases are laid for the brief "eternity" accorded to all things fashioned by mortal hands.

Brahms ever consciously schooled his imagination. He was his own severest critic. He worked slowly, produced as slowly, and, being of the contemplative rather than of the dramatic, dynamic temperamental type, he incurred the reproach of heaviness. There is enough sediment in his collected work to lend truth to this accusation, but from the very cloudiness of the ferment has come the richest of wines. And how refreshing is a draft of this wine after the thin, frothing stuff concocted at the vintage of every season! He has his metaphysical mood when he wrestles with abstract speculations, as did Pascal or Spinoza. It cannot be said that Brahms, the cryptic philosopher, is as interesting as Brahms of the symphonies, the F minor piano sonata, the quintet for piano and strings with the same key signature, or the fragrant lyrics. He has the glorious simplicity of Beethoven, and, like that Master of masters, he does not fear to employ such an elementary modulation-bridge as the chord of the dominant seventh.

A full chord for his orchestra has not the rainbow tints of the first or major chord in the Prelude to The Mastersingers, yet it can sink a shaft into our consciousness quite as profound. He is a thinker, his chilliness is rather in his manner than in his discourse, which often is thrice eloquent. This plodder, at times without Promethean fire, possesses shoulders wide enough upon which to drape the symphonic mantle of Beethoven. He reminds us of a mediæval architect whose life was a prayer, in marble; who patiently built Gothic cathedrals which majestically flanked upon mother earth, whose thin pinnacles pierced the vasty blue, and in whose marmoreal naves an army terrible with banners could worship; while through the stony forest of arches music flowed as the voices of many waters. Brahms is the master-builder of modern music.

VERDI'S OTELLO

THE announcement that Otello is to be presented by the Chicago Opera Association next
Tuesday evening at the Manhattan Opera
House is interesting to lovers of Verdi's hot-
blooded music drama. That it is not often heard
is because of the difficulty in finding singing
actors to interpret the work. Since Tamagno
and Victor Maurel, the ideal Otello and the
ideal Iago, we have had no two such interpreters.
Antonio Scotti was a remarkable Iago, and from
time to time some unhappy tenor attempts to
bend the bow of Ulysses, but the two artists
who set the town on fire twenty-five years ago
have not been rivalled. Tamagno with his bar-
baric cry, "Sangue, sangue" — "Blood, blood!"
— is unforgetable. In the killing of Desdemona he fell short of his great dramatic model,
the elder Salvini, because, as we have elsewhere
related, he left his spectators in doubt as to the
disposition of the pillow. But then his Desdemona was the lovely Emma Eames, and that,
no doubt, accounted for the indecision of the
murderous and amorous Moor at the fatal
moment.

Otello in 1887 set the musical world agog with
surprise, curiosity, and delight. It reveals little
of the narrow, noisy, violent, and vulgar Verdi

of 1850. The character drawing is by a man
who is master of his material. The plot moves
in majestical splendor and the musical psychology, especially in the case of Iago, is often subtle. Verdi has at last flowered. Much of his
earlier music, despite the admirable melodic
flow in Traviata, Rigoletto, Trovatore, smelling
ranker of the soil, showing abundant thematic
invention, was but the effort of a hot-headed
man of the footlights, a seeker after applause
and money. In Otello his musical provincial-
isms have well-nigh vanished. The writing is
clear, the passion controlled, the effects aimed at
easily compassed. The masterly craft of Iago
is cleverly contrasted with the fiery passion of
Otello, and Shakespeare is suggested; although
an Italian Shakespeare. However, the English
poet is more Italian than the Italian in this
moving drama.

Otello is veritable music drama; its composer
seldom halts to symphonize his events as does
Wagner. Arrigo Boito, most intellectual of
librettists, has skeletonized the story; Verdi's
music endows it with vitality, grace, fleshly contours, brilliancy. The Italian poet has not
gravely disturbed the original text. It is but
a compliment to his assimilation of the Shake-
spearian spirit to state that Iago's credo, an
explosion of nihilism and hatred, does not seem
out of perspective in the picture. It is an in-
tercalation of Boito's, as were the Cypriote
choruses in Act II. The rest is Shakespeare

undefiled, barring a few happy transpositions from the Senate speech to the duo at the close of Act I.

As we have said, the characterization is masterly throughout. Do not let us balk at comparisons, nor, for that matter, at superlatives. With the exceptions of Mozart and Wagner, no composer has thus far lived who could have painted the hot-blooded Moor and the cynical cannikin-clinker, set them facing each other, allowing them to work out their fates, musically speaking, as has Giuseppe Verdi. The key to Otello is its characterization. The medium in which Verdi bids his puppets of destiny to move, their fluidity, their humanity, with the complete dissection of their secret springs of action — these elements are almost incalculable. Criticism can only endeavor to disentangle them. Whether he is listening to his cunning Ancient, or caressing Desdemona, or raging like the hardy Numæan lion, it is always Otello, the Moor of Venice, a loving, suffering, living man — Shakespeare's Othello transposed to a fresco of magnificent tones.

The character does not evoke a flashy, operatic ranter. Nor does Iago, either as the bluff soldier or the loathsome serpent stinging his chieftain's soul, ever lag dramatically, ever mimic the conventional attitudes of transpontine melodrama. It is always Iago, "the spirit that denies," perhaps underlined, for music must emphasize the emotions. Desdemona is drawn in relief to her furious lover and warrior, and as a white cloud of purity in contrast with her cold-blooded maligner. Verdi has assigned her gentle music, the Ave Maria, the Willow Song. She is a sweet background upon which was etched the darker, sinister motives of the play. No masculine shadow but her lord's has been projected across her snowy, virginal soul. Delicacy and vivacity reveal, little by little, the inner workings of her girlish nature. The other figures, Cassio, Emilia, are sketches on the second plan, but figures that contribute to the density of the dramatic scheme without detracting from our interest in the protagonists.

From the opening storm to the strangling scene the music flows as swiftly as does the action of the spoken drama. Rich, varied, eloquent, the orchestra seldom tarries in its acute and vivid commentary. There is scant employment of typical motives; the kiss theme in Act I is sounded with psychologic fidelity when Otello dies. Only in the handkerchief trio is there pause for instrumental elaboration; but in the main old, set forms are avoided, and while there are melodic currents they seldom crystallize. The duo at the end of Act I, the Credo of unfaith and Otello's frenzied exhortation in Act II; the tremendous outburst in the following act, with Iago's sardonically triumphant exclamation, "Behold the lion!" as he plants his scornful heel on the recumbent Otello — then the final catastrophe — these about summarize

the high lights. Throughout there are picturesque and poignant strokes, effects of massed
splendor, and hovering about the tempest-stirred
souls is an atmosphere of gloom, doom, guilt,
and melancholy foreboding.

Verdi felt the moods of the poet and made
them live again in his score. Otello and Iago
grow before our eyes and ears from act to act.
The simple-hearted, trusting general with his
agonized cry, "Miseria mia," develops into a
ferocious savage thirsting for blood. He is the
jealous male, who sees red. The multitudinous
music is incarnadine with blood. And it is
all vocal. It is written for the voice, which is
the centre of gravity in this astounding drama of
souls bedevilled, and not the orchestra. The
pedestal is not bigger than the statue, as is the
case with Salammbô. Another such Iago, subtle, sinister, evil incarnate, withal a dangerously
attractive fellow, such an impersonation as
Victor Maurel's, may never be duplicated.
And this remarkable singing actor had the advantage of Verdi and Boito's advice when the
music drama was produced at Milan, in 1887.
Verdi's first idea of a title was Iago. This idea
does not seem strange after a performance of
Maurel.

The two most satisfying Iagos I remember
were Henry Irving and Edwin Booth. Maurel's
interpretation paralleled them at every point.
Admitted that the singing heightened the im-
pression, though it weakens the characteriza-

tion, Maurel's Iago never betrayed a tendency toward the melodramatic; as difficult as treading on eggs without crushing them, he held a middle course, and he was both a picture and a dramatic happening. Malignant he was, but that is the "fat" of the part, but he underlined the reasons for his wicked actions. Iago is also a human being with a sound motive for revenge. I know you will remind me that critical "whitewashing" is become the fashion, that Nero, Simon Magus, Judas Iscariot, Benedict Arnold, Casanova — nay, even Lucifer, Prince of Morning, has Anatole France for a defender (in The Revolt of the Angels) — are only getting their just dues at the hands of various apologists. De Quincey, a master casuist, has said that without Judas the drama of Jesus crucified would not have occurred. Everything is necessary. Nero was a much-abused monster, though Renan believes him to be the Beast mentioned in the Apocalpyse — it seems now that there were no "atrocities" during the fabulous persecutions of the Christians, that Rome was not burned by Nero, who had no fiddle technique; but in the case of Iago there is something to be said in his favor. A pure devil, as we conceive devils to be, he was not.

A rough, hard-drinking soldier of fortune, he admits himself to be, and to call his advice, "Put money in thy purse," cynical is to contravene worldly wisdom. Otello had wronged him, Iago hated him for it, hated his wife for her al-

leged infidelity — Emilia denies her treachery
— therefore, his revenge is credible. It is his
method in achieving this revenge that revolts
our sensibilities. The innocent Desdemona is
crushed between the upper and lower millstones
of inexorable destiny. Maurel did not paint his
conception all black, but with many gradations
and nuances. Not a movement but meant
something; even that famous "psychological
crook of Iago's left knee." Maurel was eco-
nomical in gesture. His was an objective characterization. The drinking song was memo-
rably, totally unlike his drinking lyrics in Don
Giovanni and Hamlet. Suffice to say that
Verdi intrusted him with the difficult task of
"originating" two such widely-sundered rôles as
Falstaff and Iago. With them Victor Maurel
made operatic history.

And now what is the most surprising thing
about Otello? I think that it is the fact that
it was composed when Verdi was past three
score and ten. This seems incredible. It
seethes with the passion of middle manhood,
with the fervors of a flowering maturity. No
one before him had dreamed of setting Shakespeare in this royally tragic fashion. Rossini
but fluted with the theme. In Verdi, jealousy,
love, envy, hatred, are handled by a master
music dramatist. It is a wonderful thing that
Verdi began it at a time when most men are
preparing for the Great Adventure. Reversing
the usual processes, this extraordinary Italian

wrote younger music the older he grew. After Aïda, Otello. After grim tragedy, joyous comedy — Falstaffio. If he had survived until ninety years, Verdi might have bequeathed us an operetta that would have outpointed in wit and sparkling humor the mercurial Johann Strauss. And when we think of the later Verdi we should not forget his faithful friend and famulus, who played Wagner to his Faust — Arrigo Boito.

FAUST AND MEPHISTO

How does Faust wear in the flicker of the footlights? Do the monologues sound with glorious resonance or are they only philosophical fustian? The question is not difficult to answer. The thunder-words of the poet-dramatist still thrill us with their meaning and with their music, the clash of souls still makes thrall of our imagination. To read Faust is to attain the summit of an intellectual peak of Darien. To witness an adequate performance of Faust is to win fresh pleasure for eye and ear. If Hamlet inspired Goethe and Marlowe before Shakespeare, his Faust in turn created a memorable literature. The very title crowds pages in encyclopædias. Sculptors chisel masterpieces after reading the poem-play; the Mephisto of the Russian Antokolsky is not easily forgotten and George Grey Barnard was inspired by the famous line, "Two spirits, alas, reside within my breast" (the group is now at the Metropolitan Museum). Painters, almost innumerable, from Ary Scheffer to the rawest art student of yesteryear have traced on the canvas the loves of Gretchen and Faust. Barbier and Carré mutilated the poem in search of effective theatrical material, and Gounod melted with sensuous ecstasy when he made the musical setting. Lenau presented a sinister, half-mad Faust, a self-portrait; the conservative Spohr surrounded the story with antiquated music. Wagner, perhaps more than other composers, realized the travailing Faust spirit in his overture, which is a masterpiece. Franz Liszt has of all men evoked within the walls of his symphonic palace both the static and dynamic Faust and the Gretchen of our dreams. His Mephisto is the cynical spirit of denial. Berlioz, as in a tremendous fresco, has painted with torrential energy the infernal glories of the theme. He even dragged his hero to Hungary so that he might give him the pleasure of hearing the Rakoczy March as orchestrated by the audacious Frenchman. Arrigo Boito, only half Latin, with Polish blood in his veins, has given us the ideal Mephisto and dared the impossible by composing the second part of Goethe's master work.

In song Gretchen has been celebrated from Schubert to the troubadour of yesterday. In romance, Turgénieff, that gentle giant, has depicted the soul of Faust transposed to Russian soil. What the Faust spirit worked in an unbalanced temperament may be noted in Nietzsche, whose later rhapsodies stemmed from Euphorion's song in the Second Part: "Let me be skipping. Let me be leaping. To soar and circle through ether sweeping is now the passion that me hath won." Therein is the kernel of the dancing philosopher, Zarathustra, who called man "a bridge connecting animal and superman." And recall the line in

Faust: "Die ird'sche Brust im Morgenrot," which served as a title for one of the unhappy philosopher's sanest books. Goethe is the matrix of modern thought; he contained Wagner as he contained Nietzsche. Wagner, of course, went to Schopenhauer for his peculiar brand of pessimism. You can't miss the Faustlike touches in Tannhäuser; the thirst for illimitable pleasure, the redemption of the eternalwomanly — all this is Faust redivivus. John Addington Symonds laments that Marlowe did not follow his Doctor Faustus with a Tannhäuser. "He assuredly would have not suffered this high mystic theme to degenerate into any mere vulgarities of a sensual Venusberg," wrote the Englishman, with one eye fastened on Wagner's version of the wonderful legend. No trivial thirst for carnal pleasures but the desire for beauty beyond human reach would have been Marlowe's conception of the brave old tale. Lohengrin is a Faust, so is Siegfried. Parsifal is Faust in the vapors of mysticism, enveloped by a Buddhistic pity; surely the "Good Friday spell" was born of that exquisite episode near the close of Act I in Faust, where the poet-philosopher gives over his contemplated suicide, ravished by sweet memories of his youth, his Sabbath wandering in spring woods and meadows.

At one time Goethe thought of translating Marlowe. His music is magical. It colored Shakespeare; it created a new dramatic school.

Marlowe is the father of English tragedy. What
if Shakespeare had died at the same age as Marlowe? "We may admit that in rhyme he never
did anything worth Marlowe's Hero and Lean-
der," says Swinburne. Charles Lamb adored
Marlowe, though he mocked the "pampered
jades of Asia." Yet the hand that fashioned
the turgid and bombastic Tamburlane also
penned that lovely lyric "Come lie ["live," in re-
vised editions] with me and be my love" (The
Passionate Shepherd). It is as sparklingly pure
as a bar of Mozart. But Marlowe is more dramatic poet than dramatist. His characters are
set forth with a mass of psychologic details
that recall some modern masters. He is an
early Browning with a mouth of gold. His
words sing. Yet he would never have written
the last speech of Paracelsus: "I press God's
lamp close to my breast; its splendor soon or
late will pierce the gloom." Marlowe was not
a believer. The desperate damnation of his
Faust chills the blood. "Where gods are not,
ghosts abound." Marlowe could surround his
unhappy hero with all the machinery of diab-
olism; Beelzebub, Prince of Flies, the Seven
Deadly Sins, imps and goblins. He could utter
that thrilling line, "See where Christ's blood
streams in the firmament," but he had not the
talent of belief — for it is both a gift and talent,
belief in the unseen. If he had with Browning's
Childe Roland to the Dark Tower come, he
would have died hopeless, impenitent, as in

reality he did die. His Faust is the archetype of the explorer in the "unplumbed, salt, estranging sea" of knowledge. He cries:

"Had I as many souls as there be stars I'd give them all for Mephistopheles." He craves eternal wisdom, "infinite richness in a little room." Mephistopheles has built for him the walls of Thebes with ravishing music. He would fain have this devil "wall all Germany with brass." He sees Lucifer, "chief lord and regent of the night," and still are his longings unassuaged. This feverish simulacrum of a man who aspired to know things terrestrial and celestial Marlowe incarnated in his tragedy.

And what horrors he conjures up in Mephistopheles's description of Hades — a description less material, nevertheless revealing a grandeur of conception second only to Dante's. This damned creature of the English poet stands for men who achieve victories or defeats by the force of their intellect. Faust summons spirits from the vasty deep, converses with them when they come, argues, even wrangles, and would circumvent them in discussion. Spiritual explorers from Giordano Bruno to Spinoza and Nietzsche are Fausts. And on the plane scientific so are Galileo and Darwin and Einstein. All who slough off decaying half-truths are Fausts who must suffer for their frankness the plagues of the world, the flesh, and the devil. Sordello's "Dante, pacer of the shore," was a mediæval Faust whose richly veined ore is half hidden in the clay of scholasticism. And so the mountains converse with mountains, Dante with Goethe, Bach with Beethoven, Marlowe with Browning.

Human insects, slowly toiling to the summits, from time to time catch glimpses of trailing cloud-glories and overhear the far-off rumblings of divine events. Then the mists part and another Faust comes to earth, telling us of the strange secrets he has surprised. "A sound magician is a mighty god," sings Marlowe. Goethe said: "Gray are all theories and green alone life's golden tree." To read Marlowe is to feel the itch of quotation. Has there ever been anything more vivid or pitiable since Dante than the English poet's Edward II, in his "cave of care," standing in mire and puddle, "and lest I should sleep, one plays continually upon a drum"? It is Chinese in its hideous suggestion of torture; we must go to Octave Mirbeau's Le Jardin des Supplices, or the newly published fiction of Charles Petit, Le Fils du Grand Eunuque, for its match. Faust is a fatalist; "his atheism has a background of terror thinly veiled by the mind's inquisitiveness." Che sarà, sarà! he declares, and then berates his satanic famulus for showing him so little. He knows that the jealous gods have somewhere buried proofs of the origin of all things, and, like Maurice de Guerin, he would have demanded: "But upon the shores of what ocean have they rolled the stone that hides them?"

BOHEMIAN MUSIC

In New Cosmopolis I called Prague the most original city in Europe, not perhaps so melodramatic as Toledo in Spain, yet quite as original, when you consider that pretty, placid Dresden is only four hours away and that further down the map lies Vienna. As the traveller approaches the Bohemian city — as Praha it is known to the natives — the cathedral and castles grouped on the hill form a fascinating silhouette against the sky-line. At once the alluring prospects of wood and architecture are evoked, and to the memory comes the sanguinary pages of its history. Arthur Symons once wrote that to a Bohemian "Prague is still the epitome of his country; he sees it as a man sees the woman he loves, with her first beauty, and he loves it as a man loves a woman, more for what she has suffered." Needless to add, for me it was love at first sight, this Prague, with its imperial palace and the Hradschin fortress so proudly perched on the Hradcany; the pinnacle of the St. Vitus Cathedral, the four Ottakan towers and the two towers of St. George, which swim so gloriously in the air, a miracle of tender rose and marble white, with golden spots of sunshine, form an ensemble that would intrigue the brush of Claude Monet.

The city proper enchants with its bewildering jumbles of architecture, its historical evocations. The Bridge of Prague, the Town Hall, the Powder Tower, the historic Tyn church, the old Jewish cemetery, the Belvedere, the Chapel of St. Wenceslas, the shrine of St. Nepomuc, the Star Hunting Lodge, where in 1620 was fought the Battle of the White Mountain, the Rudolphinium — to go on like this would send you to the guide-books. There is the modern Representatives House, where you may enjoy a symphony concert up-stairs, while in the restaurant on the first floor you can eat an omleba royal, a Fogos fish, a Telec filet specanky and Ledovy crème, ending with an Americky compôte, and — tell it not in Gath — good light wine is to be had, or the incomparable product of Pilsen, there pronounced Pizn. I stopped at the "Blauer Stern," on the Hybernska Ulice, which old-fashioned, comfortable hotel has probably changed its name since the war. Even in 1913 anything German was anathema to the Bohemians. There is the Bohemian National Theatre. Both Josef Stransky of the Philharmonic Society and Artur Bodanzky of the Metropolitan Opera House and the New Symphony Orchestra were some years ago conductors at Prague. One afternoon in the Representatives House I listened to a programme composed of national music — the Scherzo à Capriccioso of Dvorak, a symphony by Smetana, a symphonic poem by Josef Suk and a work by Sdenko Fibich, the latter a composer too little known here, whose piano compositions were introduced to us more than a decade ago by Florence Mosher and Emily Burbank at their lecture-recitals. One gray morning I went astray while wandering about the twisting corridors of the "Blauer Stern" and, tempted by the sounds of masterly violin playing, I stood before a door which bore the legend: "Otokar Sevcik." It might have been his pupils, Jan Kubelik or Kocian, though it was neither. I had seen the brilliant Kubelik at Marienbad, where I went annually to fight my fat and also to war with the rum demon — temporarily. Since then Sevcik, the great teacher of aspiring fiddlers, has removed to Vienna.

I mention these things concerning the delightful city of Ema Destinova, Thomas Masaryk — who married a New York lady, one of the Misses Garrigue of the well-known musical family; of the city wherein Mozart composed his masterpiece, Don Giovanni —"in order to express the thanks of the great master to his 'dearest citizens of Prague' for their ardent reception"; that Prague which is so dramatic to gaze upon, the Slavic city further west, the gateway to the Slavic lands — because I have just read with considerable satisfaction a slender pamphlet of fifty pages entitled The Music of Bohemia, by Ladislav Urban, published under the auspices of the Czecho-Slovak Art Clubs of New York City. The author calls his decidedly interesting contribution a sketch, but it is a sketch in which is compressed much valuable matter. At the start he tells us that "Czech" is the Slav name for the Slav people and language in Bohemia, Moravia and Silesia. The terms used to designate the whole country, the state, are 'Bohemia' and 'Bohemian.' The Czechs themselves do not employ this distinction, continues Mr. Urban, but use the word Czech in both senses. Slovaks are that people who live in the northwestern part of Hungary, called Slovakia, which with Bohemia forms the present republic and nation of the Czecho-Slovaks. Mr. Urban warns us not to confound Bohemians and gypsies, and cites Balfe's Bohemian Girl as an instance: a full-fledged Czech folk-melody is introduced as a gypsy tune in the allegro theme of the overture.

There has been bad blood between the Bohemians and Germans since the reign of King Wenceslas (921–935 A. D.). After his assassination, Wenceslas was canonized and is a national saint; a folk-song, known as the Choral of St. Wenceslas, is one of the oldest among its kind. The John Huss reformation also aroused the nation, and a battle hymn, "Ye warriors who for God are fighting," was another product of the folk. Bohemia has always been a musical nation, as Mr. Urban proves by numerous citations. Its folk-song literature is rich and varied. He quotes from Seth Watson's Racial Problems in Hungary: "Singing is the chief passion of

the Slovaks. Nothing will find its way so surely
to the heart of the Slovak people as a well-sung
song. An old peasant woman once complained
to a friend of mine that her son was a useless,
disappointing fellow. 'What was the matter?'
inquired my friend; 'did he drink or would he
not work?' 'Oh, no,' said the old woman;
'but nothing will make him sing. It's a great
misfortune.'" Rather a companionable sort,
we think — a young man who doesn't sing,
whistle or make other disagreeable noises would
be a prize in our noisy Tophet of New York.

The polka must be credited to Bohemia; it
was invented about 1830 by a country girl.
This sounds a trifle doubtful, as the dance —
called polka, rather pulka, because of the half
step — is as old as the immemorial hills of Bohemia, I have been informed by Bohemian
critics. There is a polka in Smetana's The
Bartered Bride, also a furiant, which means,
we are told, "a boasting farmer." Dvorak in
his first symphony introduces a furiant in the
place of a scherzo. But Mr. Urban is not se-
duced into that most platitudinous of errors,
to wit, that the people make a nation's music.
He writes with admirable clearness on the subject: "It is no wonder that the richness of folk-
art was overestimated in Bohemia at the beginning of the last century, and led to an error.
Folk-art was confused with nationality in art.
A false principle was constructed that 'national
art' must be based upon folk-music. Thus the

imitation of folk-poetry and folk-melodies was approved as the real national art. It is astonishing how long this principle, violating, as it did, the national law of progress, could endure. All works of this feverish, would-be-national period belong to history. They live no more, being but imitations." In a footnote to this inexpugnable statement the author adds with his accustomed acuity: "The matter was also discussed in America, where some people saw national American music under the guise of Indian music. Nothing is easier for a composer than to imitate the melodies of different nations, preserving their rhythmical or melodic mannerisms." He might have joined negro to Indian as our national, so-called, musical characteristics. But there are no more Indians, in a tribal sense, and as to negro music, the best of it was composed by white men, notably Stephen Foster. Why should Afro-American folk-tunes represent America? In MacDowell's Indian Suite there are authentic Indian themes, while in Dvorak's From the New World the negroid tunes are mere suggestions; the rhythms of Yankee Doodle are faintly heard as a contrapuntal device; in a word, the Americanism of Dr. Dvorak's plenary composition is as American as his own name, not to mention the fact that its chief motto is taken from Schubert's unfinished symphony (Tchaikovsky went to the same source for the principal theme of his E minor, the fifth, symphony, hence the accusa-

tion that Dvorak borrowed from the Russian.
Arcades ambo!) But the negro folk-tune as
a basic element for the American composer was
short-lived. Its logical conclusion landed us
in the dubious and never delectable region of
ragtime, and there let it lie forever. The musical culture of America must have its roots in
more national soil, must stem from neither the
aboriginal natives nor yet from the one-time
slaves. It must be American or it will not be at
all. At present our supreme composer is Charles
Martin Loeffler, by virtue of his individual
genius. I suspect all map-music; patriotism
may cloak humbuggery — or worse (Dr. Johnson says it does). So let us first make good
music, and the national ingredients will take
care of themselves.

Mr. Urban devoted special sections to the
chief composers of Bohemia — Bedrich Smetana, Antonin Dvorak, Zdenko Fibich, Vitezslav
Novak, and Josef Suk. There are, of course,
many others, but within the scope of his little
study these five suffice. Naturally, the palm
of superiority is awarded Smetana, whose music
we heard last season, thanks to Josef Stransky,
himself a Bohemian. Smetana is the Bohemian
composer par excellence. There is a foreign
alloy in Dvorak, especially the later Dvorak,
that rules him from entering into competition
with his fellow-countryman. Dvorak remained
a peasant even in his best works, which were
written before he came to New York in 1892.

VARIATIONS

The New World Symphony is pleasing and wears well, notwithstanding its unblushing plagiarisms — that excerpt from the Venusberg bacchanale in Tannhäuser quite takes your breath away; quotation marks are sadly needed in music! — but it remains presumably Czechish, and only faintly American. We much prefer his earlier Slavic Dances, the orchestral scherzo and the Husitzka overture. As for the newer men, it is to be hoped that Bodanzky and Stransky and Stokowski — conductors nowadays seem to be sky-high — will give them all a hearing. Quality, not quantity, rules Bohemian music, a music racy of the national soil, nevertheless not without the larger, profounder accents of universal music.

THE MUSIC OF YESTERDAY?

Notwithstanding the fact that he played the flute and ranked Rossini above Wagner, Arthur Schopenhauer said some notable things about music. Here is a wise observation of his: "Art is ever on the quest, a quest and a divine adventure;" although this restless search for the new often ends in plain reaction, progress may be crabwise and still be progress. We fear "progress," as usually understood, is a glittering "general idea" that blinds many to the truth. Reform in art is like reform in politics. You can't reform the St. Matthew Passion music or the fifth symphony. Is Parsifal a reformation of Gluck? This talk of reforms is confusing the historic with the æsthetic. Art is a tricksy quantity and, like quicksilver, is ever mobile. As in all genuine revolutions, the personal equation counts the heaviest, so in dealing with the conditions of music at the present time we ought to study the temperament of our music-makers and let prophecy sulk in its tent as it may.

One thing is certain: The old tonal order has changed forever; there are plenty of signs and wonders in the musical firmament to prove this. Moussorgsky preceded Debussy in his use of whole-tone harmonies, and a contemporary of

Debussy and an equally gifted musician, Charles Martin Loeffler, was experimenting before Debussy in a dark but delectable harmonic region. The tyranny of the diatonic and chromatic scales, the tiresome revolution of the major and minor modes, the critical Canutes who sit at the edge of the musical sea and say to the modern waves, "Thus far and no further!" and then hastily abandon their thrones and rush to safety, else to be overwhelmed — all these are of the past, whether in art, literature, music, or — let Nietzsche speak — in ethics. Even philosophy has changed its garb and logic is "a dodge," as Prof. Jowett used to say. Every stronghold is being assailed, from the "divine" rights of property to the common chord of C major.

If Ruskin had written music-criticism he might have amplified the connotations of his famous phrase, the "pathetic fallacy," for we consider it a pathetic fallacy (though not in the Ruskinian sense) in criticism to be overshadowed by the fear that, because some of our predecessors misjudged Wagner, Manet and Ibsen, we should be too tender in our judgments of our contemporaries. Here is "the pathos of distance" run to seed. The music of to-day may be the music of to-morrow, but if not, what then? It may satisfy the emotional needs of the moment, yet become a stale formula to-morrow. What does that prove? Though Bach and Beethoven built their work on the broad bases of eternity — employing that tremendous term in a limited sense; no art is "eternal" — nevertheless, one may enjoy the men whose music is of slight texture and "modern." Nor is this a plea for mediocrity. Mediocrity we shall always have with us; mediocrity is mankind in the normal, and normal man demands of art what he can read without running, hear without thinking. Every century produces artists who are forgotten in a generation, though they fill the ear for a time with their clever production. This has led to another general idea, that of transition, of intermediate types. But after critical perspective has been attained, it will be seen that the majority of composers fall into this category of the transitional; not a consoling notion, but an unavoidable conclusion. Richard Wagner had his epigones. And so had Haydn, Mozart, Beethoven. Mendelssohn was a feminine variation of Bach, and after Schumann followed Brahms — Brahms, who threatens to rival his great exemplar. Yet I can recall the incredulous smiles when, twenty-five years ago, I called the Brahms compositions "The Music of the Future."

The Wagner-Liszt tradition of music-drama and the symphonic poem have been continued with personal modifications by Richard Strauss. Max Reger pinned his faith to Brahms and absolute music, though not without an individual variation. In considering his Sinfonietta, the Serenade, the Hiller Variations, the Prologue

to a Tragedy, the Lustspiel overture, the two
concertos respectively for pianoforte and violin,
we are struck not so much by the masterly
handling of old forms as by the stark, emotional content of these compositions. It is an
error to dismiss his music as merely academic.
He began as a Brahmslaner, but he did not
succeed, as did his master, in fusing form and
theme. There is a Dionysian strain in him that
too often is in jarring discord with the intellectual structure of his work. The furor teutonicus
in conflict with the scholar. Yet at one period
Reger was considered the rival of Strauss,
though that day has long passed. Arnold
Schoenberg now divides the throne. And there
were many other claimants — Rezinek, d'Albert, Ernest Boehe, Walter Braunfels, Max
Schillings, Hans Pfitzner, Klose, Ehrenberg,
Noren, Franz Schreker, and the younger choir
whose doings are analyzed weekly by clever
Cezar Searchinger in the pages of the *Musical
Courier*. Their name is legion. They enter
the lists sounding golden trumpets of self-praise
and are usually forgotten after a solitary performance of their huge machines, whether opera
or symphony. Size seems to be the prime
requisite. Write a music-drama that consumes
three nights in its performance, a symphony
that takes a hundred men, with a chorus of a
thousand, to play and sing. Behold! You are
a modern among moderns. But your name is
as mud the following year. Exceptions are

Mahler and Bruckner, yet I have my suspicions
that when the zeal of William Mengelberg has
abated, then the Mahler craze will go the way
of all flesh, despite the fact that he has composed some thrilling pages. Otherwise, his
symphonic structures are too mastodonic to
endure; like those of Berlioz, they are top-
heavy with ennui, and many chambers are
empty of significant ideas or vital emotions.
Musical intellectualism at its extreme Kam-
chatska.

Our personal preferences incline us to the
new French music. To be sure, substance is
often lacking, but you are not oppressed by
the abomination of desolation which lurks in
the merely huge, by what Mr. Finck calls Jum-
boism in music. The formal clarity, the charming color sense, the sprightly, even joyful, spirit,
combined with an audacious roving among
revolutionary ideas, all endear these youngsters
to us. Debussy is their artistic sire, Ravel
their stepfather, and if d'Indy does not fall into
this category, being a descendant of Franck,
he is none the less admirable as a musician.
Stravinsky outpoints them all in the imprévu,
as does the incredible Prokofieff — a man to be
carefully estimated, one who thus far hasn't
put his best foot foremost in America. The
Richard Strauss case is no longer a moot one.
He has in all probability given his best work,
and superlative work it is, despite its slag, scoriæ,
rubble, and refuse. He is the chief of a school,

a position from which he can never be dislodged, and when history sifts the pretensions of all the second and third rate men of his generation, his figure will be found standing close to Wagner's and Berlioz's and Liszt's. An epigone? Yes. But an epigone of individual genius.

With Arnold Schoenberg freedom in modulation is not only permissible but an iron rule; he is obsessed by the theory of overtones, and his music is not only planned horizontally and vertically but in a circular fashion. There is in his philosophy no such thing as consonance or dissonance, only perfect ear training. (We quote from his Harmony; a Bible for Supermen). He writes: "Harmonie fremde Tone gibt es also nicht"— and a sly dig at old-timers — "sondern nur dem Harmonie-system fremde." After carefully listening to his "chaos" a certain order disengages itself; his madness is methodical. For one thing, he abuses the interval of the fourth and he enjoys juggling with the chord of the ninth. Vagabond harmonies in which remotest keys lovingly hold hands do not dissipate the sensation of a central tonality somewhere — the cellar, on the roof, in the gutter, up above in the sky so high. The inner ear tells you that his D minor quartet is really thought, though not altogether played, in that key. As for form, you must not expect it from a man who has declared: "I decide my form during composition only through feeling," a procedure which in other composers' works might be called improvisation. Every chord is the outcome of an emotion, the emotion aroused by the poem or idea which gives birth to the composition. Such antique things as the cyclic form or community of themes are not to be found in Schoenberg's bright lexicon of anarchy. He boils down the classic sonata form to one movement and begins developing his theme as soon as it is announced. We should be grateful that he announces it at all; themeless music is the rage at present.

So, as it may be seen, the new dogmatism is more dogmatic than the old. The absence of rule in Schoenberg is an inflexible, cast-iron law of necessity as tyrannical as the Socialism that has replaced Czarism with a more oppressive autocracy, the rule of the unwashed, many-headed monster. Better one tyrant than a million. There is no music of yesterday or to-morrow. There is only the music of Now.

LISZT'S ONLY PIANO SONATA

THAT two young American-born pianists, John Powell and Louis Cornell, should have selected recently Liszt's only piano sonata for their programmes, and during the same week, is sufficiently significant to call for comment. It is a sign of the times. Many of the innovations in modern writing for the instrument may be directly traced to this same B minor sonata, and when we name it as the composer's solitary excursion into the classical domain, it is with full consciousness that Liszt's "fantasia quasi-sonata," after a reading of Dante, in Années de Pèlerinage, is hardly to be described as a sonata. What is a sonata? Liszt answers the question in his highly original work. He rejects the old order of three or four separate movements, substituting a more complete organism. It may not be, formally speaking, the Haydn, Mozart, or early Beethoven sonata. Liszt employs as a spring-board the last sonatas of Beethoven to launch him into novel territory (study opus 110 in A flat and you will recognize the truth of this contention).

Charles Souilier has declared that the sonata expired with the eighteenth century, which gave it birth. This is a rather risky statement. If true, we should have missed such beautiful music in the form — Schumann, Chopin, Brahms, Liszt. The Hungarian's astonishing use of the leading-movement and its metamorphosis, one theme of the slow introduction, as Shedlock, in his book on The Pianoforte Sonata, is the source whence he derives the principal part of his tone picture, and, adds Mr. Shedlock, "everything depends on the quality and latent power of the fertilizing germ." But on the first page of the B minor sonata may be found Wotan's chief theme, the scream of Kundry, and a color scheme which Wagner later incorporated in the Ring and Parsifal. So the "fertilizing germ" is not missing. As for the form, that is easily discernible. Liszt has spun a complex web, his sonata is an arabesque, and a logical one, for nothing is more inexorably logical than a seemingly loose rhapsody. The chief fault of this composition is not its form or lack of melodic invention, but its length — it demands at least thirty-five minutes to play — caused by repetitions, though in different keys, thus defeating the very purpose for which it was composed, i. e., suppression of unnecessary episodes and breaks in the continuity. The same criticism holds good for the Symphonic Poems.

Liszt's influence was not only profound upon his contemporaries — witness Wagner — but on the latter-day school, headed by Richard Strauss, whose tone poems are inconceivable without Liszt's discoveries. He also inspired the Russians, and his impressionism is the base of

Debussy and Ravel's piano music. Rimsky-Korsakoff we long ago christened the Russian Berlioz, yet he owes Liszt more; from Berlioz he learned how to paint orchestrally, but in his manner of composition he leans heavily on the Hungarian. Sadko comes from Liszt's symphonic poem, Ce qu'on entend sur la montagne, while Antar and Scheherazade come from Harold and the Faust symphony. As a French critic has written: "The brand of Liszt remains ineffaceable" on those charming works of Rimsky-Korsakoff. Like Moses, Liszt saw the Promised Land, but was destined never to enter it. He suffered the fate of intermediate types. He was recognized too late. Dr. Frederick Niecks, the biographer of Chopin, has wisely said: "Be, however, the ultimate fate of his works what it may, there will always remain to Liszt the fame of a daring striver, a fruitful originator, and a wide-ranging quickener."

The eminently pianistic quality of Liszt's original music commends it to every pianist. Joseffy told the present writer that the B minor sonata was one of those compositions that plays itself, it "lies" so beautifully for the hand. No work of Liszt, with the possible exception of his études, is as interesting. Agreeing with those critics who declare that they find few traces of the sonata form in the structure, and also with those who assert the work to be an organic amplification of the old obsolete form, and that Liszt has taken Beethoven's last sonata period

as a starting-point for his plunge into futurity —
agreeing with these warring factions, we find
fascinating music in this sonata. What a dramatic work it is! It stirs the blood. It is intense. It is complex. The opening bars are
truly Lisztian. The gloom, the harmonic haze
from which emerges that bold theme in octaves
(Wotan's theme), the leap from C to the A
sharp below — how Liszt has stamped this and
the succeeding intervals as his own! Power
there is, sardonic power, like the first phrase of
the E flat piano concerto, so cynically mocking.
How incisively the composer traps your consciousness in the theme of the sonata, with its
four knocking D's! What follows might be a
drama enacted in the netherworld. Is there a
composer who paints the infernal, the macabre,
with more suggestive realism than Liszt? Berlioz and Saint-Saens and Raff come to the mind
as masters of the grisly and supernatural. But
the thin, sharp flames of hell hover about the
brass, wood-wind, and shrieking strings in the
Liszt orchestra.

The chorale, usually the meat of the Lisztian
composition, now appears and in dogmatic
affirmation proclaims the religious belief of the
composer; our convictions are swept along until
after that outburst in C major, when follows the
insincerity of it all in the harmonic sequences.
Here, surely, it is not a whole-hearted belief,
only theatric attudinizing; after the faint return of the first motive is heard the sigh of sen-

timent, of passion, of abandonment, which engenders the suspicion that when Liszt was not kneeling in prayer he was prostrate before woman. He blends piety and passion in the most mystically amorous fashion; with the cantando expressivo in D begins some lovely music, secular in spirit, mayhap intended by its creator for reredos and pyx.

But the rustle of silken attire is behind every bar; sensuous imagery, a delicate perfume of femininity lurks in each trill and cadence. Ah! naughty Abbé, have a care! After all thy tonsures and chorales, thy credos and sackcloth, wilt thou admit the Evil One in the guise of a melody, in whose chromatic intervals lie dimpled cheek and sunny tresses! Wilt thou permit her to make away with thy spiritual resolutions? Vade retro me Sathanas! And behold it is accomplished. The bold theme, so triumphantly proclaimed at the outset, is now solemnly sounded with choric pomp and power. Then begins the hue and cry of diminished sevenths, and this tonal panorama with its swirl of intoxicating colons kaleidoscopically moves onward. Again the devil tempts our musical St. Antony, this time in octaves and in the key of A major. He momentarily succumbs, but that good old family chorale is repeated, and even if its orthodoxy is faulty in spots it serves its purpose; the Satan is routed and early piety breaks forth in an alarming fugato, which, like the domestic ailment known as a bad conscience, is happily short-winded. Another flank movement of the Eternal Feminine, this time in the seductive key of B, made mock of by this musical Samson, who in stretta quasi presto views his weakness with contrapuntal glee. He shakes it from him, and in the bass triplets frames it as a picture to weep or rage over.

All this finally leads to prestissimo finale of startling splendor. In the literature of the piano there is nothing more exciting. It is brilliantly captivating, and Liszt the Magnificent is painted on every bar. What gorgeous swing and how the very bases of the musical anvil tremble under the sledge-hammer blows of this tonal Attila. Then follow a few bars of the Beethoven-andante, a moving return to the earlier themes, and softly the first lento descends to the subterranean abode, whence it emerges, a Magyar Wotan, majestically vanishing not in the mists of Valhalla but in the bowels of Gehenna; then a genuine Lisztian chord-sequence followed by a profound stillness in the major. The B minor sonata displays Liszt's power, Liszt's weakness. It is rhapsodic, it is too long — infernal, not a "heavenly length" — it is noble, drastic, cerebral, and it is blazing with exotic hues. It is also cynical and insincere. Liszt, more than other composers, Meyerbeer and Berlioz excepted, excelled in depicting a sneering, cynical sensuality. Also insincerity. And when you come to think it over, it takes genius to suggest in tones the insincere. This

feat Liszt achieved. In his symphony to Faust
he succeeds better with the Mephisto picture
than in his characterization of Marguerite. But
to deny the B minor sonata a commanding position in the Pantheon of piano music would be
folly. And interpreted by an artist saturated
in the Liszt tradition, such as Arthur Friedheim
— who has intellectual power and never resorts
to mere sentimentalism — the work almost com-
passes the sublime.

Away from the glitter of the concert-room
this extraordinary Hungarian, inspired after the
loftiest in art, yet in the atmosphere of aristocratic salons, or of the papal court, Liszt was
not altogether admirable. We have heard certain cries calling heaven to witness that he
was anointed of the Lord (which he was not);
also that if he had not cut and run to sanctuary
to escape the petticoats — one was his egregious
Polish Princess — we might never have heard
of Liszt the Abbé. This theory is not far from
the truth. Among the various penalties under-
gone by genius is its pursuit by gibes and glos-
saries. Like Ibsen and Maeterlinck, the composer Liszt has had many things read into his
music which do not belong there. He set great
store by his sacred compositions, his masses and
his psalms, and he was bitterly disappointed
because Rome did not espouse his reforms in
churchly music, notwithstanding his close friendship with Pope Pius IX. But there is a vein
of insincerity running throughout this music,

despite its ecclesiastic pomp and operatic coloring. Perhaps the best estimate of Franz Liszt is the purely human one. He was a virile musical genius, and was compact of the usual pleasing and unpleasing faults and virtues as is any great man not born of a book.

DREAMING OF LISZT

PHILIP HALE once wrote that they buried
Richard Wagner in the back yard like a cat;
which is irreverent yet a bald statement of the
fact. Liszt is also buried at Baireuth, in a for-
lorn pagoda designed by his grandson, Siegfried
Wagner, who, at the time of his grandfather's
death, was a student of architecture. After a
pilgrimage to this tomb in the cemetery in the
Erlangerstrasse, for I count myself among the
Lisztianer, and also after hearing several operas
of Siegfried I reached the conclusion that, notwithstanding critical opinion to the contrary,
the young man wisely abandoned his architectural dreams. But it is another kind of
dream that I would describe this Sunday morning. When a young chap, I was crazy to see,
to hear, Liszt, and while I think that the old
man with long white hair and warts on his face
was the real Liszt — I met him on the Rue de
Rivoli in 1878 — still the possibility of a closer
view haunted my sleeping and waking hours,
and, finally armed with letters of introduction
from a well-known French pianist, a pupil of
the musical Merlin, and a Paris music publisher,
I found myself one evening at the Gare de l'Est,
en route for Strasburg, thence to Stuttgart,
and Weimar. In those times, forty years ago,
we travelled slowly.

DREAMING OF LISZT

A lovely morning in May saw me walking through a sun-smitten lane on the road to the garden-house where his Serene Highness was living. I had sent my introductions to the royal household the previous evening. I had been summoned. The hedges were white with spring blossoms, the air redolent of bockbier. Ah! thronging memories of youth. Suddenly a man on horseback, his face red with excitement, his beast covered with lather, dashed by, shouting, "Make way for the Master. He comes. He comes!" Presently a venerable being with a purple nose — a Cyrano de Cognac nose — appeared, and walking. His hair streamed in the wind. He wore a monkish habit, and on his head was a huge shovel-shaped hat of the pattern affected by Don Basilio in The Barber of Seville. "It must be Liszt or the Devil," I cried, and the only Liszt smiled, his warts growing more purple, his expression most benignant. He waved to me a friendly hand, that formidable hand, which, like a steam-hammer, could crush steel or crack the shell of an egg, so sensitive was it. "Both Liszt and the Devil," he grunted, and then I knew my man. I kissed his hand, made the sign of the cross, for I was addressing an ecclesiastic, an Abbé, though one without a tonsure, and created a deacon by Pope Pius IX, called Pio Nono in Italy, but in Rome affectionately nicknamed "Pianino" because of his love of piano music, Liszt's in particular.

He invited me to refreshments at the Czerny Café, but as it was crowded we went across the street to the garden of the Elephant Hotel, there to be surrounded by a throng of little Liszts, pupils, male and female, who mimicked the old, old gentleman in an absurd manner. They wore their hair on their shoulders, they sprinkled this hair with flour, they even went so far as to paint purplish excrescences on their chins and brows. They donned semi-sacerdotal robes, they held their hands in the peculiar style of the Master; they, too, sported shovel-shaped hats, and from time to time they indulged in patibulary gestures. But, good Lord, how they could down the beer!

Enfin, after some diplomatic skirmishing I was invited to the afternoon musicale and went with the gang to the pretty little home of Liszt in the ducal park. Liszt was amiable. He knew that I was nervous, so he asked a few promising young beginners, such as Arthur Friedheim, Alfred Reisenauer, Moriz Rosenthal, Emil Sauer, Richard Burmeister, to open the ball. After I heard them I wished myself in Buxtehude. I had proclaimed myself as an ardent upholder of the Thalberg school, which champions a singing touch and pearly scales. I had studied all the Thalberg fantasies on operatic airs with Charles H. Jarvis of Philadelphia, who could read prima vista any music composed by man, god, or devil. You will estimate my musical and intellectual equip-

ment of those days when I tell you that my
battle-horse was the Prayer from Moses in
Egypt, arranged by Thalberg, and my favorite
reading the prose of Chateaubriand; in few
words, lush, luxuriant, and overblown romanti-
cism. The step to Ouida's novels and the Hen-
selt études was not far. All that I detest now in
music and literature was then my passion. Like
Ephraim I was sealed to my idols, and the chiefest was Thalberg, natural son of Prince Lichten-
stein, a handsome piano virtuoso with aristocratic side-whiskers, a smooth pianistic style,
and a euphonious touch.

Liszt called to me. "Tiens! let us hear some
music by an admirer of my old friend Sigismund
Thalberg." I did not miss the veiled irony of
the speech, the slight underlining of "friend,"
for I had read of the historical Liszt-Thalberg
duel in Paris during the third decade of the
last century. But memories soon annulled my
agony. What a via dolorosa I traversed from
my chair to the piano — by the way, a Steinway concert-grand. I shall not forget to my
dying hour that chamber wherein I stood the
most fateful afternoon of my life. Liszt, with
his powerful profile of an Indian chieftain,
lounged in the window embrasure, the light
streaking his hair, silhouetting his brow, nose,
and projecting chin. He was the illuminated
focus of a picture that is burnt into my memory
cells. The pupils were wraiths floating in a
misty dream, with malicious points of light for

eyes. I, too, felt like a disembodied being in this spectral atmosphere of which Liszt was the living reality.

Urged by a hypnotic will I went to the piano, sat before it, and in my nervous misery lifted the fall-board and paused to decipher the name of its maker; that's how I discovered Steinway. My act did not pass unperceived. Whispering ensued, followed chuckling, and some one said: "He must have begun as a piano salesman." It was the voice of the witty Rosenthal, and it utterly disconcerted me. Facing me on the wall was Ary Scheffer's portrait of Chopin, and doubtless prompted by the subject, my fingers groped among the keys and I began, without rhyme or reason, the weaving prelude in D of the immortal Pole. My insides were shaking like a bowl of disturbed jelly, though outwardly I was as calm as growing grass. Oddly enough my hands did not falter, the music seemed to ooze from my wrists. I had not studied in vain Thalberg's Art of Singing on the Pianoforte. I finished. Not a murmur was heard. Then Liszt's voice cut the sultry air: "I had expected Thalberg's tremolo study," he casually remarked, avenging himself with an epigram on his old rival a half century after their battles. But Thalberg didn't hear it. I did. I took the hint and bowed myself out of the royal presence, permitted by the boss to kiss his technique-laden fingers, and without stopping for my hat and walking-stick in the ante-chamber I went away.

Then tempted by the cool of the woods I strayed across to Goethe's Garden House. At the moment I preferred poetry to music. Nevertheless, I had played for Liszt. Rotten playing, of course, yet a historical fact. But when I compiled a life of the Grand Old Man of Hungary I hadn't the courage to put my name in that long list of reputed pupils, though I dare say I didn't play any worse than some of them. · Ask Arthur Friedheim.

My hat and stick I sent for. I was not precisely in a jubilant mood, though I joined the Liszt lobby that night at the Hotel "Zum Elefanten." It was a goodly crowd, the majority of whom achieved musical fame later. In the Weimar of those days Liszt walked and talked, smoked big black cigars, drank his share of brandy, played, composed, and prayed — he seldom missed early mass. Despite his Hungarian origin, his early French training, there emerged through the palimpsest of his brilliant and complex personality the characteristics of his mother, an Austrian born. He loved German music, German ways. He liked to speak that tongue in preference to French. Of the Magyar language he knew little. But his music is Hungarian enough; Hungarian in the sense that Tchaikovsky's is Russian — *i. e.*, cosmopolitan. However, there's a lot of nonsense written about that fetish of a certain critical school, the fetish of nationalism in music. Liszt would have been invincibly Liszt even if he had been born in Boston. And that tropically passionate town does not in the least resemble Budapest.

At the Liszt museum his old housekeeper Paulina Apel — I must ask Albert Morris Bagby if she still lives — showed me its numerous memorials. What a collection of trophies, jewels, manuscripts, orders, pictures, letters, and testimonials from all over the globe. I read a letter from Charles Baudelaire to Liszt, which is not to be found in the volume dedicated to his correspondence. Gifts from royalty abound. In glass cases are the scores of Christus, the Faust Symphony, Orpheus, Hungaria, the Berg Symphony, Totentanz, and Festklaenge. Besides the Steinway in the music-room there was an old instrument dating back to the forties; for the little piano upon which he studied as a child you must go to the Budapest museum. At Weimar may be seen marble hands of Liszt's, Beethoven's, and Chopin's; also the long, nervous, spider-like fingers of Liszt clasping the slender hand of the Princess Sayn-Wittgenstein. Like Chopin, Liszt attracted princesses and other exalted personages in petticoats as does sugar buzzing flies.

And then I woke up. I had been dreaming in my Parisian attic in 1878. When I went for the first time to Weimar in 1896 Liszt had been dead ten years.

A BRAHMA OF THE KEYBOARD

In a half-forgotten study of Flaubert's masterpiece, L'Education Sentimentale, which he rightly calls A Tragic Novel, George Moore compares the great Frenchman to Brahma "creating the passing spectacle of life to relieve his eternal ennui." . . . Now, Leopold Godowsky is not Brahma, and he has never suffered from ennui, thanks to his tremendous capacity for work; yet I can't help picturing him as a sort of impassive Asiatic deity seated before the keyboard of his instrument calmly surveying the eternal spectacle of music and its many masques. All schools, all styles, he knows, but upon this vast knowledge he has no desire to make any personal comment. Passionless, passionate, objective and subjective, his crystal-clear comprehension of the musical universe has made him apparently assume the attitude of an omniscient spectator, though he is neither one nor the other. Louis Ehlert asked Karl Tausig — probably the greatest of all piano virtuosi — why he did not offer up a small sacrifice to the human needs of the masses. The Pole replied: "I am not sentimental; neither my life nor my education intended me to be so." Ehlert persisted. "How would it be if you were to give us an historical representation of the sentimental?" he suggested. Tausig shook his head and shrewdly smiled. He never made concessions to public taste, and he was called inhuman, cold, objective. His master, Liszt, was the reverse, overflowing with the milk of human music, spontaneous and prodigal in his play. Tausig the obverse of the medal; yet I believe that Liszt and Tausig were the piano Dioscuri, and not Liszt and Chopin. Chopin as a pianist has a niche all his own.

In an article several years ago and in the magazine section of *The Times*, I wrote that Leopold Godowsky is a pianist for pianists, as Shelley is a poet for poets. But everybody reads Shelley nowadays, and no doubt compares him unfavorably with the ear-splitting verse of the cacophonous young poets of the hour. Leopold Liebling took exception to my ascription, and I fancy he is right; every musical person listens to the alluring playing of Godowsky quite impervious to the fact that there are aspects of his art which will always escape them. In his playing he is transcendental. This doesn't mean that he is frostily objective; he is human, emotional, and has at his finger ends all styles. It is the fine equilibrium of intellect and emotion that compels our admiration. No one plays Chopin like Godowsky, no, not even that tricky kobold, Vladimir de Pachmann. Paderewski is more emotional, Josef Hofmann extorts a richer, a more sonorous tone from the wires; nevertheless, Godowsky is a Chopinist in a class apart. He doesn't drip honey in the nocturnes as does Ignace Jan, Premier of Poland; he can't thunder the polonaises like his friend Jozio from Cracow; but these qualities he gives us in his own scale of tonal values. He is a powerful man with muscles that are both velvet and steel. When he wishes he, too, can sound the orchestral note; but, then, he seldom wishes this. His feeling for the limitations of the piano recalls the words of Rafael Joseffy: "I'm not a brass band"; Joseffy, who, in his abhorrence of a smeary touch produced his legato with the aid of the pedals, and what an aristocratic floating touch was his! What poetry! What atmosphere!

Setting aside his Chopin interpretations, which we take for granted, as he is Slavic, have you heard Godowsky play Mozart, or the neglected Haydn; or Schubert, Schumann? Of his Bach, Beethoven, and Brahms I shall not write. I can only repeat — all schools are at his beck, and if they are "perfect pictures, perfectly framed and hung," as Joseffy said of his beloved master, Tausig, there is also the personal equation, for me, full of magic. Sensationalism, the pianistic fracas, posing for the gallery, all the bag of cheap tricks this great pianist eschews. He is master of the art of playing the piano beautifully. His exquisitely plastic phrasing, artistic massing of colors, above all the nobility of his conception — little wonder I call him a Brahma of the keyboard, far-fetched as the simile may sound. To Godowsky all other pianists could go to school, if for nothing else but the purity of his style, his kaleidoscopic tintings, his polyphony. And it must be admitted that pianists I have spoken to about him admit his power. He does not boast the grand manner of Josef Hofmann, yet Hofmann is reported to have told his manager that he enjoyed listening in a room to Godowsky more than playing to crowded and enthusiastic multitudes at his own concerts. Truly a fraternal and noble sentiment! If it comes to sheer sensationalism, then Godowsky easily leads them all, Rosenthal not excepted. I refer you to his paraphrases of Chopin, Weber, and Johann Strauss, and the supreme ease with which he conquers them. Brahma, indeed. Although as he plays he looks more like Buddha under his Bodh tree conjuring beautiful sounds from sky and air and the murmuring of crystalline waters.

It must be nearly twenty years ago, anyhow eighteen, that I entertained Vladimir de Pachmann in my Dream Barn on Madison Avenue at Seventy-sixth Street. The tenth floor, a room as big and as lofty as a cathedral. Alas! where are such old-fashioned apartments to-day? After eating a duck, a kotchka, cooked Polish fashion, and borsch, beet soup, with numerous Slavic side-dishes, preceded by the inevitable zakuska—those appetite-slaying bonnes bouches —De Pachmann fiercely demanded cognac. I was embarrassed. Not drinking spirits, I had inconsiderately forgotten the taste of others. De Pachmann, who is a child at heart, too often a naughty child, cried to heaven that I was a hell of a host! He said this in Russian, then in French, Italian, German, Polish, Spanish, English, and wound up with a hearty Hebrew "Raca!" which may mean hatred, or revenge, certainly something not endearing. But the worst was to come. There stood my big Steinway concert grand piano, and he circled about the instrument as if it were a dangerous monster. Finally he sniffed and snapped: "My contract does not permit me to play a Steinway." I hadn't thought of asking him, fearing Chopin's classic retort after a dinner party at Paris: "Madame, j'ai mangé si peu!" Finally I saw the hole in the millstone and excused myself. When I returned with a bottle of abominable cognac the little man's malicious smile changed to a look of ecstasy, and he was not a drinking man ever; but he was accustomed to his "petit verre" after dining, and was ill-tempered when deprived of it. Such is human nature, something that Puritans, prohibitionists, and other pernicious busybodies will never understand. And then this wizard lifted the fallboard of my piano and, quite forgetful of that "contract," began playing. And how he did play! Ye gods! Bacchus, Apollo, and Venus and all other pleasant celestial persons, how you must have revelled when De Pachmann played! In the more intimate atmosphere of my apartment his music was of a

gossamer web, iridescent, aerial, an æolian harp
doubled by a diabolic subtlety. Albert Ross
Parsons, one of the few living pupils of Tausig,
in reply to my query, How did Joseffy compare
with Tausig? answered: "Joseffy was like the
multicolored mist that encircles a mighty mountain; but beautiful." So Pachmann's weaving
enchantments seemed in comparison to Godowsky's profounder playing.

And what did Vladimir, hero of double-notes,
play? Nothing but Godowsky, then new to me.
Liszt had been his god, but Godowsky was now
his living deity. He had studied, mastered, and
memorized all those transcendental variations
on Chopin studies, the most significant variations
since the Brahms, a Paganini scaling of the heights
of Parnassus; and I heard for the first time the
paraphrase of Weber's Invitation to the Valse, a
much more viable arrangement than Tausig's;
also thrice as difficult. However, technique, as
sheer technique, does not enter into the musical
zone of Godowsky. He has restored polyphony
to its central position, thus bettering in that respect Chopin, Schumann, and Liszt. I have
called attention elsewhere to Godowsky's solo
sonata, which evokes images of Chopin and
Brahms and Liszt — only in the scherzo. Instead of exhuming such an "ungrateful," un-
pianistic composition as Tschaikovsky's Sonata
in G, pianists of caliber might more profitably
introduce the Godowsky work. He is too modest or else too indifferent to put it on his programme. It "lies" so well for the keyboard,

yet there is no denying its difficulties, chiefly polyphonic; the patterns are intricate, though free from the clogging effects of the Brahms sonatas. De Pachmann delighted his two auditors from 10 P. M to 3 A. M. It is safe to wager that the old Carrollton never heard such music-making before or since. When he left, happy over his triumph — I was actually flabbergasted by the new music — he whispered: "Hein! What you think! You think I can play this wonderful music? You are mistaken. Wait till you hear Leopold Godowsky play. We are all children, all woodchoppers, compared with him!" Curiously enough, the last is the identical phrase uttered by Anton Rubinstein in regard to Franz Liszt. Perhaps it was a quotation, but De Pachmann meant it. It was the sincerest sentiment I had heard from his often insincere lips. We were all three surprised to find a score of people camping out on the curved stairway and passages, the idealist, a colored lad who ran the elevator, having succumbed to sleep. This impromptu Godowsky recital by a marvellous pianist, for De Pachmann was a marvel in his time, must have made a grand hit with my neighbors. It did with me, and when Godowsky returned to New York — I had last heard him in the middle nineties of the previous century — I lost no time in hearing him play in his inimitable manner those same works. A pianist who can win the heartiest admiration of such contemporaries as De Pachmann and Joseffy and Josef Hofmann — I could adduce many other names — must be a unique artist. And that Godowsky is.

When he isn't teaching or playing with orchestra or in recitals Mr. Godowsky spends his leisure in pedagogic work. There is a wide-spreading education scheme which has St. Louis as headquarters, the name of which I've forgotten, though the name doesn't much matter, as musicians the country over know it. For this Mr. Godowsky is editing the classics and romantics of piano literature. He is also composing the most charming music imaginable for the earlier and middle grades of students; music that has genuine musical values, with technical. Imagination and instruction blended. Pegasus harnessed to the humbler draught horse. If you think of Schumann's various albums for the young you may surmise the spirit of the Godowsky curriculum. I have been reading through his Miniatures for four-hands (Carl Fischer, New York), three suites, twelve numbers in all, in which the treble is for the pupil of extreme simplicity yet demanding attention to the melodic line, and amply developing the rhythmic sense. With their fanciful titles, tiny mood-pictures, these Miniatures are bound to attract all teachers of the instrument. Leopold Godowsky is a master pedagogue, as well as a master of masters among virtuosi. He belongs to the race of such giants as Paganini, Liszt, Tausig — and he is "different."

CONTEMPORARY BRAN

YESTERDAY was housecleaning in my office, which I need hardly tell you is situated under my hat. The principal débris to be removed and dumped into the waste-paper basket were letters addressed to this department. Their number was appalling, the accumulation of weeks, as the music editor has little time for answering letters. A dozen concerts a day, opera almost every night, do not make for the life tranquil. Now, letters, anonymous or signed, are always interesting, especially those in the first category. Praise and blame run neck and neck; cinquante-cinquante, in classic parlance. Occasionally abusive missives arrive, breathing fire and fury, and these are of psychologic import. You ask yourself why? And lose yourself in an interesting labyrinth of speculation. The small boy who chalks naughty words or figures on wall spaces during the spring of the year testifies to the rising sap of the budding season; it is an outlet for his nascent emotions. Presumably this is the case with those whose handwriting reveals their uneasy sex. But why do they select the present incumbent of this chair of criticism? William James, when he dissected Dr. Nordau, twenty-five years ago, pointed out as a major symptom of the too

critical Max what is called by psychiatrists co-
prolalia, or a tendency to indulge in vulgar,
abusive language. When certain inhibitions of
polite society are removed the patient indulges
in vile speech, and writes nasty and usually
anonymous letters for reasons only known to
himself or herself. Writers of anonymous letters are described as cowardly, but this is only
half the truth; they are also sick-brained, suffering from mild hysteria, and as soon as they trans-
fer to paper the expression of their petty spite
are temporarily relieved; there is "a load off
their minds," as they put it.

This doesn't mean that all anonymous letters
are abusive; some of them are pleasant reading.
A blushing maiden records her admiration. A
"violinist" tells me that I have overpraised
Raoul Vidas, although I was not at the concert
in question, Sunday being my day of respite
from the boiler shop; now and again pertinent
criticism is received, but, whether signed or un-
signed, all these communications only prove that
their recipient's casual writing is closely read,
and that is a minor consolation. Then there are
the letters asking for advice, and these contain
harder nuts to crack. Why warn a young man
or woman that musical criticism as a profession
is a delusion and a snare? Neither one will believe you. Why suggest to an ambitious young
composer that any other avocation will bring
him, if not happiness, then, at least, bread and
butter? But the stone hankers after the star,

and who shall mock its aspiration? How often
have we felt like crying aloud: "Hats on, gentleman, this is not a genius!" reversing the historic utterance of Robert Schumann. A critic
should be clairvoyant, but sometimes he is not.
And little wonder. Paste passes for diamonds,
skim-milk masquerades as cream. But it is
always well to face the rising, not the setting
sun. Write only for young; the old will not
heed you, being weary of the pother of life and
art. To the young belongs the future. Hurrah
for Ornstein and Prokofieff, or the ideals they
represent! Progress always traverses a circle,
it is more imaginary than real, but we must have
the illusion of progress, else spiritually decay.
Without vision people perish. Nice copybook
axioms, paste them in your bonnet.

In Emile Hennequin's La Critique Scien-
tifique — introduced to English readers by John
Mackinnon Robertson in his New Essays
Towards a Critical Method — the brilliant
Frenchman, unhappily dead before his time,
advanced the idea that every critic should, in
the preface of his book, set forth not only his
qualifications, but also his prejudices, his limitations. This procedure might shed a dry light
on what follows, although it would seem unnecessary, as all these virtues and defects are
implicit in the critics' work. However, Mr. Robertson has elaborated the theory and frankly
exposes himself. I am minded of this by a
signed letter, evidently written by a gentleman,

which came to this department shortly after a notice had appeared criticising the Oratorio Society. The critic, it seems, must have been in a disgruntled humor when he declared that the oratorio form was as obsolete as the mastodon, or some other prehistoric monster; perhaps he meant hippopotamus. The writer of the communication protests, and logically, against sending a man to criticise choral singing when he is not in sympathy with such. Other people, numerous people, find in oratorio the musical staff of life. Why, then, trample on their feelings? The answer is an unqualified assent to the argument. As I signed the criticism in question, and as I was bored to death at the time, there is nothing left for me but to apologize — also put on paper my objections, thus following the advice of the distinguished French critic. And I fear I shall make out a poor case for the defense.

In the first place, on the night of the Oratorio concert, our oratorio editor, yielding to a perfectly human impulse — about the fourth time in his life — accompanied the sporting editor to a marvellous wrestling match between El Greco, the Terrible Greek (his real name is said to be Theototocopulous), and Goya, better known as the Man-Strangler. Which one first went to the mat on that tremendous occasion need not concern us now; suffice to say that I was butchered to make the oratorio editor's holiday. Why do I dislike oratorio? I meekly retort — I don't. I love it, and my correspondent is right

when he asserts that the form has served as a
vehicle for most masterly music. Think of
Bach, Handel, Mendelssohn. I know it. I
have heard and loved choral singing for a half
century. Masterpieces never weary, but, as
Arthur Symons says, books about books soon
pass away, and there are some of us who prefer
to read than "see" Hamlet, although I agree
with Brander Matthews that the only test of a
play is "the fire of the footlights." In a word,
public performance may rob the masterpiece of
its original grandeur — and we must predicate
grandeur for the B minor Mass, for the Messiah,
for Elijah. This sounds as if I were about to
lay the blame on the particular performance of
the Oratorio Society — a cowardly evasion of
my duty. On the contrary, I confess that with
the exception of the inevitable limitations of
amateur singing — Signor Setti choruses are not
plentiful — I had never heard the Oratorio Society sing with such refreshing vigor as the week
before last. Remember, too, that I heard the
society under Leopold Damrosch, when it sang
The Damnation of Faust at the Academy of
Music, Philadelphia, and young Walter conducted a chorus in the wings.

You will ask, You love the noble music in this
form, why write deprecatingly of it? Because
it is my unshakable conviction that such music
does not belong in the concert room, but in a
church. After hearing the Passion music in
Bach's old St. Thomas's Church, or the Brahms

Requiem in a historical church, the anomaly of singers in festive array singing in concert halls is too much for my sense of eternal fitness. Yes, critics have "nerves," and it needs a remarkable interpretation of the Messiah or kindred compositions to stir me. I am only answering for myself — qui s'excuse, s'accuse? — and do not presume to gainsay the feelings of pious folk who regard the Messiah as a sacred function. But for those who tell me that the mock-turtle Christianity of Parsifal is "sacred" I merely retort: "A fig for the mystic capon." Naturally, a concert room better serves the practical purpose of singing organizations here than the house of God; yet I prefer the church, for the spectacle of five hundred humans, with their mouths wide open bawling the text — would it not distract one? Sacred fiddlesticks! you exclaim when a tenor, faultlessly clad, arises and solemnly intones, "And Jesus said," the remainder of the speech being uttered by some one else. Æsthetically, oratorio has not a leg to stand on. It is neither fish nor flesh. How dull was Samson et Dalila till sung in costume and before the footlights! And it is not by any means very dramatic. Still, to many who do not visit the opera for religious reasons, oratorio is a species of emotional outlet. It is a half-way house, a compromise — you may enjoy both drama and religion. Another thing — I am weary of the music, as I weary when I see Hamlet or hear the Fifth Symphony, or look at the Dresden Madonna. I am not apologizing for this weakness, only trying to explain its genesis. William Gillette has written about the "first-time" element in acting; or why an actor must ceaselessly renew the freshness of his original inspiration. Would that some sympathetic writer deigned to take up the cudgels for the ear-sick music critic. It is difficult, nay, impossible, to recapture that first rapture when Tristan, or the C minor Symphony, or Hamlet, swam into our ken. That is why I did not "react" the other night at the Oratorio Society, and why, as my critique was reprehensible, I am now making a clean breast of the matter and crying: Peccavi!

And here is my old friend Frank Sealey mildly complaining that it was not his fault that his electric organ "ciphered" for a bar during the evening. As I have literally sat at Brother Sealey's feet for nearly thirty years — since the opening of Carnegie Hall — it is not necessary to assure him that I never doubted that it was the fault of the organ, not his. He is a rock of certitude on the organ bench. But I did enjoy Wolf-Ferrari's Vita Nuova, a beautifully fashioned score, too sweetly sentimental in spots for the austere and lovely sonnets of the deathless Dante; nevertheless, a tour de force, happily illustrating my primal contention that the oratorio form is as obsolescent as the epic; the spirit, I mean, rather than the form, for the bony framework is there, but the age of piety, the profound piety that prompted the composition of such glorious music as Bach's or Handel's, has quite vanished, to be replaced by machine-made music, the "movies," and other stimulating arts. Contemporary bran is filling, but it nourishes not the soul. Need I add, when the Oratorio Society sings the Messiah at Christmas-tide, that the regular oratorio editor, a singularly pious person, will report the annual occurrence! That night, perhaps, I shall enjoy the brutal but diverting spectacle of a wrestling match. It all depends on the amiability of the sporting editor.

A MOOD REACTIONARY

I CONSIDER such phrases as the "progress of art," the "improvement of art," and "higher average of art" as distinctly harmful and misleading. How can art improve? Is art a something, an organism that is capable of growing into a fat maturity? If this be so, then, by the same token, it can become a doddering, senile thing, and finally die and be buried with the honors due its useful career. It was Henrik Ibsen who asserted that the vital values of a truth lasted at the longest about twenty years; after that the particular truth rolled into error. Now, isn't this quibble concerning "artistic improvement" as fallacious as the vicious circle of the dramatist from the Land of the Midnight Whiskers — or is it the Land of the Midnight Bun? Contrariwise, Bach would be dead, Mozart moribund, Beethoven in middle-aged decay. Instead, what is the musical health of these three composers? Have we a gayer, blither, more youthful scapegrace writing to-day than Mozart? Is there a man among the moderns more virile, passionate, profound, or noble than Beethoven? And Bach is the boy of the trinity. The Well-Tempered Clavichord is the Book of Eternal Wisdom. In it may be found the past, present, future of music. It is the Fountain of Eternal Youth.

VARIATIONS

As a matter of cold fact, it is your modern who is ancient; the ancients were younger. Recall the Greeks and their naïve joy in creation. In sorrow the twentieth-century man brings forth his art. His music betrays it. It is sad, complicated, hysterical, morbid. No need to mention Chopin, who was neurotic — an empty medical phrase — nor Schumann, who carried in him the seeds of madness; nor Wagner, who was a typical decadent on an epical scale. Sufficient for the argument to adduce the names of Berlioz, Liszt, Tschaikovsky, and Richard Strauss. Some Sunday when the weather is wretched, when icicles hang by the wall, and "ways be foul" and "foul is fair and fair is foul," I shall tell you what I think of the "blond barbarian" who sets to music crazy philosophies, bloody legends, sublime tommyrot, and the pictures and poems of his friend. At present I am not in the humor nor have I the space. Good white paper is become a luxury, like freedom of speechlessness and other indelicacies of the national cuisine.

As I understand the jargon of criticism, Berlioz is the father of modern instrumentation. That is, he says nothing original or significant in his music, but he says it magnificently. A purple, pompous rhetorician, a Chateaubriand of the orchestra. His style covers a multitude of musical — or unmusical — defects with the flamboyant cloak of chromatic charity. He pins haughty, poetic, high-sounding labels to his compositions, and, like Charles Lamb, we sit open-mouthed at concerts trying to fill in his big, sonorous, empty frame with an adequate picture. Your picture is not the same as mine. I swear that the young man who sits next to me, with a silly chin, goggle eyes, and a cocoa-nut-shaped head, sees as in a flattering mirror, the idealized image of a strong-jawed, ox-eyed, classic-browed youth, a mixture of Napoleon and Byron. I loathe the music that makes its chief appeal to the egotism of mankind, all the while slyly insinuating that it only addresses the imagination. Yes, the imagination of your own splendid ego in a white waistcoat driving a new model car through the White Light district on an immoral afternoon in the puberty of spring.

Let us pass to the Hungarian piano virtuoso, who posed as a great composer. That he lent his hard cash and musical themes to his precious son-in-law, Richard Wagner, is undeniable. Liszt admits it himself. But, then, beggars must not be choosers, and Liszt gave Wagner mighty poor stuff at times. We believe that Wagner liked far better the solid shekels than the notes of hand. Liszt would have had little to say if Berlioz had not preceded him. The idea struck him, for he was a master of musical snippets, that Berlioz was too long-winded — both in brass and wood — that his so-called symphonies were neither fish, nor form, nor good red tunes. What ho! cried Master Franz, I'll give them a dose homœopathic. He did, and he named his prescription Symphonic Poem, or, if you will, Poème Symphonique, which is not the same thing. Nothing so tickles the vanity like this sort of verbal fireworks. "It leaves so much to the imagination," murmurs the fat man with a 22-collar and a No. 6 hat. It does. And his kind of imagination — good Lord! Liszt, nothing daunted because he couldn't shake out an honest throw of a tune from his technical dice-box, proceeded to build his noise on so-called themes, claiming that in this method he derived from Bach. Not so. Bach's themes are subjects for fugal treatment, Liszt's are used symphonically. The parallel is uncritical. Besides, Daddy Liszt had no melodic invention. Bach had, and in abundance; witness his chorals, masses, oratorios, preludes, suites, fugues. However, the Berlioz ball had to be kept a-rolling; the formula was easy. Liszt named his poems, named his very notes, put dog-collars on his harmonies — yet no one whistled after them. Whoever whistled a Liszt tune?

Tschaikovsky kept one eye on Liszt and Berlioz, the other on Bellini and Gounod. What would have happened if he had been one-eyed I cannot pretend to say. In love with lush, sensual melody, infatuated with the gorgeous pyrotechnical effects of Berlioz and Liszt, also the pomposities of Meyerbeer, this Russian, who began too late in his studies, succeeded in manufacturing a number of ineffectual works. On

them he bestowed strained, fantastic titles,
empty, meaningless, pretty, and as he was con-
trapuntally short-winded, he made his so-called
tone-poems shorter than Liszt's. He had little
aptitude for the symphonic form, and his development section is always his weak point.
Too much Italian sentiment, and a sentiment
that is often hectic and morbid. He raves or
whines like the people in Russian fiction. I
think he was touched in the upper story, that
is, till I heard the compositions of R. Strauss of
Munich. What misfit music for such a joyous
name, a name evocative of all that is gay, witty,
sparkling, spontaneous in music. After Mozart,
give me Strauss — Johann, not Richard.

No longer the wheezings, gaspings, short-
breathed phrases of Liszt. No longer the sensuality, loose construction, formlessness and
vodka besotted peasant dances of Tschaikovsky,
but a blending of Wagner, Brahms, Liszt — and
the classics. Richard Ostrich knows his little
affair. He is clever, he is skilled. He has his
chamber-music moments, his lyric outbursts.
His early songs are singable. It is his vile,
perverse orgies of orchestral noises that wound
my ears. No normal man ever erected such
mad architectural tonal schemes. He should be
penned behind the bars of his own mad music.
He lacks melody. He dotes on ugliness. He
suffers from the uglification complex. He writes
to distracting, unheavenly lengths, worst of all,
his harmonies are hideous. But he doesn't for-

get to call his monstrosities fanciful names. If it isn't Don Juan — shades of Mozart — it is Don Quixote — shades of Cervantes. This literary title humbug serves as the plaster for our broken heads and split eardrums. Berlioz, Tschaikovsky and R. Strauss are not for all time.

The truth is that musical art has gone far afield from the main travelled road, has been led into blind alleys and dark forests. If this art has made no "progress in fugue, song, sonata, symphony, string quartet, oratorio, opera," who has "improved" on Bach, Handel, Haydn, Mozart, Gluck, Beethoven, Schubert, Schumann, Chopin? Name, name, I ask. What's the use of talking about the "higher average of to-day?" How much higher? You mean that more people go to concerts, more people enjoy music, than fifty or a hundred years ago. Do they? I doubt it. Of what use all our huge temples of worship if the true gods of art no longer be worshipped therein? Numbers prove nothing. Majorities are not always in the right. There has been no great original music composed since the death of Beethoven, for, strictly speaking, the music-drama of Wagner is a synthesis of the arts, and, despite his individual genius, in union there is death — in the case of the Seven Arts. United we fall, divided we stand! The multiplication of orchestras, opera-houses, singing societies, and concerts are not indicative that general culture is achieved.

Quality, not quantity, should be the shibboleth. The tradition of the classics is fading, soon it shall vanish. We care little for the masters. Modern music worship is a fashionable fad. People go to listen because they think it the mode. Alack and alas! that is not the true spirit in which to approach the Holy of Holies, Bach, Handel, Mozart, and Beethoven. Oremus!

MUSICAL "POTTERISM"

Potterism is a clever, amusing satire on the British philistine which has had considerable vogue in London and New York. It was written by Rose Macaulay, who is said to have a dozen novels to her credit. The lady has evidently read Shaw profitably; that is, Nietzsche strained through the Shaw sieve, for G. B. S. never had an original idea. She defines Potterism as a frame of mind, not a set of opinions. Potterism is only a new word for an old thing — cant, or, as we say, humbug, and, on its more serious side, hypocrisy. Smug self-satisfaction is its keynote. Will Irwin in a flash of divination defined the particular quality as "highbrow," a species of sterile intellectualism which irritates sensible people because of the lofty, condescending attitude assumed by certain persons who, terribly at ease in Zion, are seemingly in the secret councils of the Almighty. Don Marquis daily tilts at æsthetic sham in his stimulating Sun Dial column, and Gelett Burgess, the author of the deathless Purple Cow, long ago hit out at the Potterism of his time. Potterism, like the rich, is always with us. We are all of us more or less Potterites. Dickens painted the tribe, beginning with Mrs. Leo Hunter, not forgetting Podsnappery. Thackeray's scimitar prose cut through snobbish pretenses, while a

French philosopher, Jules de Gautier, in his
Bovaryisme, has demonstrated that we are
victims of the world illusion — to pretend to
be otherwise than we are. It is a law of life,
a superstition, this game of self-illuding, and
superstition is the cement of civilization.

Therefore, Miss Macaulay has dealt with
nothing novel, but she has written an agree-
able variation on the theme of human weakness, and the most engaging quality of her formula is its elasticity. No matter the department of life, Potterism lurks thereabouts.
Musical Potterism, for example, is everywhere
rampant. It bobs up in music criticisms and
peeps forth in daily intercourse. "Give me
good old Mozart," cries the classical Potterite,
"and keep your modern kickshaws. Mozart
is good enough for me!" Alas, we think Mozart is too good for this bonehead, who no doubt
prefers a Broadway comic opera to The Marriage of Figaro. Another of the exasperating
Potterites is the haunter of concert halls who
spends his time in comparing violinists, pianists,
singers, orchestras. Criticism thrives on comparisons. That we know; but the infernal hair-
splitting over this bald subject gets on your
nerves. Music and morals is another favorite
grouping of two widely sundered things. Not
so, asserts the uplifter who seeks sermons in
running Bachs and usually finds immoral rubble. Of all the damnable nuisances in the Vale
of Tone, commend me to your moralizer. He

249

is too much in evidence nowadays, and his pernicious influence will, I feel certain, close every theatre, opera-house, picture-gallery, and book in our present United States of Slaves.

There is too much critical cant concerning the classics of music. How uncritical we are! We say Mozart and Beethoven just as we say Goethe and Schiller. Such bracketing is bubbling bosh. It is almost Hegelian in its identification of opposites. We can understand the conjunction of Mascagni and Leoncavello in Cavalleria and Pagliacci, a managerial marriage, with our eye on the box office. But Bach and Beethoven. Or Schumann and Chopin. How absurd and lazy-minded is such association of names! One of the most ingrained of Potterisms is that the gallery at the opera is the repository of the most precious criticism. For gallery, read the standees at our opera — the rail birds, so called. As a matter of fact, the most illegitimate applause comes from these quarters. Does a tenor bawl, a basso bellow, a soprano scream, thunderous explosions prove our contention. When Galli-Curci sang off key at the Lexington Theatre last season she was hailed in an unmistakably cordial manner. We have noticed the same lack of taste at the San Carlo, Naples; at La Scala, in Milan; in Paris, Berlin, and London. Italian audiences, especially of the top gallery, are supposed to possess finer ears than other people. More musical Potterism. They applaud in Italy, as they applaud in New York or London, the singers with the stentorian or extremely high voices; whether they sing in tune or not, whether they rhythmically distort the musical phrase or not, matters little to these fanatics for noise. And invariably they drown the orchestra if the singer happens to end a few bars before it. That the composition should be allowed to terminate logically does not enter into their unmusical comprehension. To bruise their muscular palms and shout is their idea of sensibility. We do not refer now to the official claque, if there be one at the opera, but to the diabolical hand-clapping and hurrahing which is becoming a formidable menace to the enjoyment of the musical portion of the audience. No applause is tolerated during Parsifal until act-ends, no applause is tolerated at Tristan and Isolde until the curtain falls, and what a relief it is not to be forced to endure the belching enthusiasm and vulgar fist-thumping in the middle of a musical phrase! Why, then, are not Italian and French operas given the same chance? We are indeed barbarians in this cult of noise. We can't even escape noise within our opera-house. It would be a wise regulation if applause could be confined within legitimate limits — at the end of each act. It might not please some singers, who are so avid of applause that they actually hire it by the yard, but it would be a boon to the occupants of the stalls and boxes at the Metropolitan. Hasta la vista!

We blush to utter such Potterisms. There should be no necessity for these obvious criticisms. Another annoying Potterism is the growing hero-worship of conductors — nothing rare, by the way, in the history of art. We remember Theodore Thomas in his palmy days; remember that smoothly fitting dress coat of his. Yes, there were many women who attended the Philharmonic Society concerts to gaze ecstatically upon the shapely back and harmonious movements of this handsome conductor. Another prima donna conductor was Arthur Nikisch of the Boston band. He waved lily-white hands; his weaving motions fascinated the eye. They seemed in their rhythmic variety the externalization of the music he was interpreting, and, according to Delsarte and Dalcroze, they were. But both Thomas and Nikisch were great conductors — Nikisch still is; indeed, he is the dean of great conductors. His personal mannerisms were and are taken as a matter of course. We do not include Arthur Bodanzky among the prima-donna baton heroes. Nevertheless, he is a hero, and a hero always in a hurry. He is the most precise and businesslike of our conductors. He seems as if he were making a train to Eldorado. Yet it is only a fancy. He is absolutely master of his technical and intellectual resources. The enormous dynamic energy of the man, his driving power, are concentrated at the tip of his stick. If the Boston Symphony Orchestra boasts a demon drummer, the National Symphony Orchestra can boast a demon conductor. Bodanzky is demoniacal when he cuts loose. At the second Tristan performance he galloped his men at such a pace that the singers could only pant after them. A great conductor is Artur with the Weber profile and the propulsive right hand. If he had a calm left hand like Thomas or Nikisch his readings would benefit thereby. But how stimulating is his conducting! You swing along on the crest of exaltation and forget the composer's intentions in the tumultuous symphonic sea. A brilliant apparition, a stork of genius, but with brains, always brains. The dark horse of American conductors is Ossip Gabrilowitsch. That young man will bear watching.

His antipodes is Walter Damrosch, who is as familiar a spectacle nowadays as Trinity Church. Walter leaves nothing to chance. He doesn't believe in the imprévu; with him the unexpected never happens. There is a sense of security at his Symphony Society, the sort of security that appeals to you when sitting under a long beloved preacher. Since 1881, on and off, we have sat metaphorically at the feet of Walter Damrosch, and not once has he startled, not once has he altogether disappointed us. He is safe, sane, and — sometimes — soporific. But he never uses rouge or pencils the eyebrows of his interpretations; perfume is to him abhorrent. Good old Walter! His has been a long race, and his a sober victory. Leopold Stokowski is a pocket edition of Nikisch, a Nikisch without genius. He is the ideal primadonna conductor and exudes sweetness and light (Einstein says that light exudes), and as regards the technique of the baton he has all his contemporaries beaten to a frazzle — save one, Arturo Toscanini. Such economy of gesture, such weighty significance in every motion are praiseworthy. His musicianship is excellent, his memory remarkable, although commanding intellectuality is absent. He too has a sinuous line in his back that enchants his feminine audience. He is graceful, and inevitably makes his entrance carrying his bâton as if it were a baby. The Philadelphia Orchestra is largely composed of mediocre material, but thanks to the admirable disciplinarian, that is, Stokowski, it sounds at times as if of prime quality. And tonal quality is precisely what it lacks. Its conductor hypnotizes his audience into thinking it is so. Ah, these Poles! The Oriental mango magic trick over again. Stokowski is young, blond, and has a Chopinesque head, but in profile his chin is as diffident as a poached egg. Pierre Monteux, like a happy nation, has no personal history. He is an accomplished chef. We enjoy his cuisine. There is a savory touch of the Midi in his musical ragouts. And to my horror I find myself indulging in the most reprehensible musical Potterism.

MY "CHILDE ROLAND"

IF you keep good company too long it is difficult to remain a decent member of society. This sounds like a faded paradox, but I mean it. No doubt vaso-motor reflex action is the cause. Try it yourself. Frequent the abodes of the self-righteous, of prohibitionists, of reformers and uplifters generally, and you will soon crave moral wood-alcohol, possibly the more vicious benzine. Too much opera drives me back to the church, and thence to the House of the Flesh where the spirit sleepeth. Because he was a clergyman's son and brought up in a moral straight jacket, dosed with moralic acid, Friedrich Nietzsche exploded such a phrase as "Christianity, alcohol — the two great means of corruption" to civilization. I have often wondered why he dragged in rum? (This is a variant on Whistler's epigram.)

However, I'm not attempting unimaginary conversations, nor describing insurrections in oyster-shells. A Scotch proverb warns us: "Never tell your foe when your foot sleeps"; nevertheless I shall make a confession that involves both feet, also my sleeping cortical cells. The good company mentioned above chiefly consisted of young, ambitious composers, an approved gang of musical chaps who delighted in symphonically setting poetic ideas, whether from Byron, Nietzsche, Ben De Casseres, or d'Annunzio. And when I say symphonically I mean symphonic poems, for the great symphonists were long ago voted by this coterie as "old stuff." Liszt and Richard Strauss were our springboards. The Debussy influence was yet to come. It was Tchaikovsky who most appealed to us. Realism, not imagination, was our shibboleth. As all my friends were composing I took it into my head to go them one better, to be more realistic than the ultra-realists. I had, so I fancied, the necessary science. I consulted young Henry Hadley, who was quite a promising lad at that time, and he advised — after putting me through a course of contrapuntal sprouts — to go ahead and do my worst, which worst would only mean spoiling music-paper, while my best — ! Who knows?

I fancied that I had mastered the tools of my trade, that I knew every form from a song to a symphony, and that my scoring comprised the entire gamut of orchestral pigments — you see, false modesty didn't stand in the way — so I began to cast about for my poetic subject and its musical counterpart, hoping — such is the audacity of youth — that the appearance of the pair would be simultaneous, as in the dual-composing of Richard Wagner. I didn't expect much, did I? Well, one fine night, as I wearily tossed on my folding bedouin, my musical imagination began to work. I remember now that it was a spring night, the moon rounded, lustrous, and silvering the lake beneath my window. I had been re-reading for the hundredth time Childe Roland to the Dark Tower Came, from my favorite poet, Robert Browning, with its sinister coloring, its spiritual overtones. Yet until that moment it had never suggested musical treatment. Perhaps it was the exquisite cool of the night, its haunting mellow atmosphere, that fermented in my brain-box. I went to the window. Suddenly I saw a huge fantastic cloud shadow project a jagged black pattern on the water. Presto! I had my theme. It came with an electric snap that blinded me for an instant. It would be the first motive of my symphonic poem, Childe Roland. It was thought in the key of B minor, a key emblematic of the dauntless knight who to "the dark tower came," unfettered by enemies, physical or spiritual.

How my imagination seethed the night through, as I am one of those unhappy men who, the moment an idea comes to them, must develop it to the bitter end. Childe Roland kept me on tenterhooks till dawn. I heard the call of his "dauntless horn," and saw the "squat tower." The knight's theme, so it seemed to me, was Roland incarnated in tone. I overheard its underlying harmonies with the instrumentation, all sombre, gloomy, the note of gladness missing. I treated my theme with vitality, announcing it on the English horn, with a strange rhythmic background supplied by the tympani; the strings in division played tremolando, the brass was staccato and muted. It was novel enough to me, although this description must sound banal to modern ears. After seven months of agonizing revision, pruning, clipping, cutting, and hawking it about for the inspection of my friends, and getting laughed at for my pains, I finished the unwieldy work. But the performance! Diplomacy won the day. A music-critic, who could compose a symphonic poem was more of a rarity in those far-away days than now, when children make fugues while you wait. There was an interview with Herr Kapellmeister Schnabelowsky and a definite promise. I shall spare you details of the seventeen rehearsals, hours and hours in duration, when my amateurish orchestration was held up to scorn by the conductor for the delectation of the band (though I always paid for his beer at Lüchow's). The audience at the concert had the pleasure of reading in the programme-book the entire poem, Childe Roland, no doubt wondering what it meant. My symphonic poem would make clear the dark, dubious sayings of the poet. I believed then in the power of music to portray definite soul-states, to mirror moods, to depict, though indefinitely, common every-day physical facts.

My composition was adequately played, of that there was no doubt. Give the Herr Kapell-

meister his due. It was only ninety minutes
long — remember it was a symphonic poem,
not a symphony — and I sat in nervous perspira-
tion as I listened to the Childe Roland theme,
to the squat tower theme, the "sudden little
river" motive, the horrid engine of war motive,
the sinister grinning false-guide theme, in short,
to the many motives of the poem with its tremendous apotheosis, ending with the blast from
the slug-horn of the dauntless knight. I hope
you are acquainted with this extraordinary
poem, for I have met confirmed Browningites
who had never read it. After Paracelsus and
Sordello it is my daily sustenance. The apotheosis theme I sounded with twelve trombones,
twenty-one basset horns, one calliope and a
chorus of one thousand two hundred, with a
vacuum choir for celestial coloring. It almost
brought down the roof and I was the happiest
person in the audience. As I went away I encountered an old friend, the critic of The Disciples of Tone, who said to me:

"Mon cher maître, I congratulate you, it
beats Richard Strauss all hollow. Who and
what was your Childe Roland? Was he any
relative of Byron's Childe Harold? No, yes,
no? I suppose the first theme represented the
'galumping' of his horse, and that funny tri-
angular fugue meant the horse was lame in one
leg and going it on three. Adieu! again con-
gratulations. I'm in a hurry." He fled. Tri-
angular fugue! Why, that typified the cross-

roads before which Childe Roland hesitates. How I detested that unimaginative critic! I was indeed disheartened. Then I was saluted by a musical lady:

"It was grand, perfectly grand, but why did you introduce a funeral march in the middle? You know in the poem Childe Roland is not killed till the end." I thanked her with a wry face. The funeral march she alluded to was not a march but the Quagmire theme, that quagmire from which queer faces threateningly mock at the brave knight. Hopeless, thought I, musical people have no imagination. In the morning newspapers I was treated rather roughly. I was accused of cribbing my opening theme from the overture to The Flying Dutchman, and giving it a rhythmic twist for my own ends — as if I hadn't conceived it on the spur of an inspired minute! I was also told that I couldn't write a fugue, that my orchestration was overladen, my part-writing crooked, while the work as a whole was deficient in symmetry, development, repose, above all in coherence. This last was too much. If Browning's poem was pictured in my music, why, then, Browning was to be blamed for the incoherence, not I. I had faithfully followed his poetic narrative. Years later, when I became a member of the critical guild, I saw in a clearer light the reasons for those divagations. You can't fool all the critics all the time.

Months afterward I read in his book, The

Beautiful in Music, by Edward Hanslick, that "Definite feelings and emotions are unsusceptible of being embodied in music." So I had been on a false track. Charles Lamb and Hanslick had reached the same conclusion by diverse roads. I realized that my symphonic poem Childe Roland told nothing to its hearers of Browning's poem; that my own subjective and overthrown imaginings were not worth a rush; that as music the composition had objective existence, though not as a poetical picture, which must be judged on its musical merits alone; its themes, development, formal excellence, and not because of its arbitrary fidelity to a literary programme. When I set about analyzing, I discovered what poor stuff I had produced; how my fancy had tricked me into believing that my half dozen heavily instrumented themes, with their restless migrations into many tonalities were "souls and tales marvellously mirrored," when they were nothing of the kind.

In reality my ignorance of form, and lack of contrapunted knowledge, had made me label the work a "symphonic poem"— an elastic, high-sounding, pompous, and empty tithe. In a spirit of revenge on my fatuity I rearranged the score for small orchestra and it is now played in the circus under the better understood name of The Patrol of the Night-Stick, and the critical press has particularly praised the graphic power of the night-stick motive and the verisimilitude of the quick "get-away" of the burglars in the elaborate coda. Alas! poor Childe Roland.

If our young composers would study Hanslick's book much good might accrue. It is all very well to give your composition a grandiose title, but do not expect that your audience will understand your idea. We may be thinking of something quite different, according to our respective temperaments. I may enjoy the formal musical side; my neighbor, for all I know, will, in imagination, have buried his rich, irritable old aunt; therefore your pæan of gladness, with its clamor of brazen trumpets, means for him the triumphant ride home from the cemetery and the anticipated joys of the post-mortuary baked meats and the subsequent jag. You never can tell.

"OSCAR" AND DVORAK

WELL I remember the day when Oscar Hammerstein first entered the office of the *Musical Courier* and introduced himself to Editor Marc A. Blumenberg. The year may have been 1888, perhaps 1889. He told Mr. Blumenberg that he was worth a million dollars, which sum he had made from a patent cigar-cutting machine; he also said that he was the editor of a trade journal devoted to the tobacco industry. Blumenberg looked at me, winked, and shook his head. The future impresario, with that ironical smile of his, noticed the incredulous movement and asked: "You think I'm meshugah? I'll prove that I'm not crazy," and he produced irrefragable evidence that he was neither crazy nor poverty-stricken. He was worth more than a million, and Marc immediately became interested. Who wouldn't have? Oscar was then dreaming of opera in English. The failures of American operatic companies had only blazed a trail for him, a trail that would be bound to end in success. He thought that good singing in our native language at moderate prices would solve the problem. Every experimenter starts out with that simple thesis, a dangerous one, as opera has little to do with art, music, good singing, or vernacular speech.

Opera is an exotic. It is a fashionable function or nothing. Oscar was told this by Blumenberg, but he in turn shook his head. He
proposed to be another Columbus and show
them the egg trick. He had a hundred predecessors, and no doubt he will have a thousand
successors. But somehow the egg never stands;
that is, in English.

There was much pow-wowing between the
two editors that I can't recall. The less I understand a libretto the more I enjoy the music.
I agree with Harry B. Smith, who has said that
when an opera is a success the composer gets
the credit; when a failure, the blame is saddled
upon the book. As the librettist of Robin Hood
and a string of other De Koven and Smith
operas, Mr. Smith knows what he is talking
about. W. S. Gilbert was in the same rocking
boat with Arthur Sullivan. Later, Oscar Hammerstein was to settle the question by writing
both words and music for The Kohinoor, thus
patterning after Richard Wagner. But at first
he was rather timid. I don't believe he took
Blumenberg's advice, or, indeed, the advice
of any one, except Campanini's. Opera at the
Harlem Opera House followed after an interval.
It was not an enlivening affair. When I read
in some obituary articles that Hammerstein had
engaged Lilli Lehmann, Schumann-Heink, Al-
vary, Fischer, and others for his One Hundred
and Twenty-fifth-Street season, I also shook my
head. I can't remember such an imposing ar-

ray — as they say in funeral notices — at the old Harlem Opera House. Does any one? I remember the burning mountain in Auber's Masaniello, or The Dumb Girl of Portici (what a film it would make, this dumbness), and there were other mediocre revivals, not worthy of critical consideration.

However, Oscar was not to be discouraged. He proceeded to play the game with energy and recklessness. He was a gambler born. Organizing opera companies, vaudeville shows, erecting opera-houses in New York, Philadelphia, London, building theatres, playing with men and millions, what were the achievements of Henry E. Abbey or Colonel Jack Haverly compared with those of this shrewd, ever-witty, good-tempered Hebrew, who was more prodigal with his own money than other managers were, and are, with the capital of strangers?

Hammerstein's original operetta was once upon a time as celebrated as his hat. The composition was the result of a wager made by Oscar and Gustave Kerker, the composer of The Belle of New York, Castles in the Air, and a dozen other popular pieces. Kerker is a well-trained musician, and, naturally, he was rather sceptical when Oscar boasted of his musical genius. Whatever gifts Oscar may have possessed, modesty was not one of his failings. I have heard him quote with gusto Goethe's dictum as to the modesty of fools. At a table one afternoon a quarter of a century ago, at the old

Gilsey House, in the café, sat Oscar, Kerker,
Charles Alfred Byrne, dramatic critic and librettist; Henry Neagle, then dramatic editor of the
New York Recorder — since defunct — and the
present writer. Taunted by some one, Oscar
became excited and offered to compose an opera,
words and music, within forty-eight hours.
Gus booked the bet — the amount of which I've
forgotten. Rooms were engaged in the Gilsey,
an upright piano installed, and, cut off from the
world, Hammerstein began tapping out tunes
— he was a one-fingered virtuoso — scribbling
verse, and altogether making himself extremely
busy. I forgot to say that Gus Kerker had
agreed to orchestrate the masterpiece.

Then we had lots of fun. Louis Harrison
engaged a relay of hand-organs to play under
the composer's windows, but Oscar never winced.
The hotel authorities had to telephone the police
in order to get rid of a string of Italian piano-
organists passionately grinding out popular melodies on Twenty-ninth Street. Plates of sinister ham sandwiches were sent to his room, accompanied by a brigade of cocktails. And the
tray was always returned empty, with the composer's thanks. I've forgotten the other pranks
we played, and all to no purpose. Complaints
were made at the hotel office that a wild man
was howling and thumping the keyboard; again,
uselessly, for, barricaded, the composer refused
to give up the fort. Exhausted, but smiling,
Oscar at the end of the allotted time invited the

jury on awards to listen to his music. It proved a tuneful hodge-podge, also proved the composer's retentive memory. Every operetta composer was represented. The book was a joy. It would have pleased little Daisy Ashford. (Why doesn't some humor-loving musician set The Visiters to music?) Kerker threw up the sponge. He had to pay the bet. The curious side of the affair is that the operetta was actually produced at the New York Theatre a few months later, reinforced by extra numbers, considerably "edited," and it met with some success. To be sure, the composer was also the owner and manager of the three theatres clustered under one roof. That first night of The Kohinoor was not only notorious, it was side-splitting. The audience, of the true Tenderloin variety, laughed themselves blue in the face. I can only recall that the opening chorus consumed a third of the first act. Oscar knew the art of camouflage years before the word was imported. Two comic-stage Jews alternately sang, "Good morning, Mr. Morgenstern; good morning, Mr. Isaacstein," while the orchestra shifted the harmonies to avoid monotony. I fancy that was a device of Kerker's. Oscar "composed" a second operetta, but it never achieved the popularity of The Kohinoor.

During a certain period the Hammerstein hat was without duplicate, except that worn by William M. Chase, the painter. Nevertheless, the Hammerstein hat was unique, not alone for the gray matter it covered, but because of its atmospheric quality. It was a temperamental barometer. When the glass had set fair the tilt of the hat was unmistakable. If storm clouds had gathered on the vocal horizon the hat registered the mood and righted itself like a buoy in agitated waters. Its brim settled over the eyes of its owner; his people flurried into anonymous corners. Or else the hat was pushed off his forehead: unbuttoned then his soul. You might dare to approach and beg for seats. A weather gauge was Oscar's hat. Ask his one-time famulus, W. J. Guard. He knew. Or Mary Garden. Oscar had hurled his hat at her head in the long ago. What a brim it had, this hat. Oh! the breadth and flatness thereof. How glossy its nap, in height how imposing. To have described Hammerstein without his hat would have been as disastrous as to give the Ring without Wotan. Shorn of it the owner would have been like Alberich sans Tarnhelm. As an Irishman would have said: His hat was his heel of Achilles. Oscar sported it while sleeping. Inside was stencilled the wisdom of Candide: "Il faut cultiver notre Jardin." (Mary, of course.) Many painters yearned to portray that hat in Oscar's dome of action. The impressionists would have painted it in complementary tones; the late William M. Chase would have transformed it into a shiny still-life. George Luks would have made it a jest for Hades; Arthur B. Davies would have changed it into a symbol — the old Hebraic chant, Kol Nidre, might have been heard echoing around its curved surfaces, as echoes the Banshee on a funereal night in dear old Tipperary. It was a hat cosmopolitan, alert, joyous, both reticent and expensive. It caused a lot of people sleepless nights, did this sawed-off stovepipe with its operatic airs. Why did Oscar Hammerstein wear it? For the same reason that a miller wears his hat, and not for tribal or political reasons. Requiescat in Oscarino! Pardon my Latin.

But Oscar musical? Oscar a man of fine musical tastes or intelligence? Basta! He had the native wit to select as General for his operatic army a skilled conductor and a musician of judgment and vision. That is the reason New York had such a wide and novel repertory offered to it at the Manhattan Opera House. When Signor Cleofonte Campanini left Hammerstein his musical fortunes began to wane. But as a dynamic driving force I cannot name his equal, except Jack Haverly, or Barnum.

When I was on the professional staff of the National Conservatory — the only musical institution in this country that deserved the appellation — I was intrusted by the President, Jeannette M. Thurber, with the care on his arrival of Dr. Antonin Dvorak, Bohemian composer and musical director of the Conservatory. For the "man in the street" his name means his

Humoresque as played by the inimitable Fritz Kreisler, or wheezed out by some unmusical instrument of torture; canned music; in the consecrated phrase of Arthur Whiting, "musical waxworks." But Dvorak also composed The New World symphony, and other trifles; these, however, do not trouble or soothe the digestion of table d'hôtes. With "Old Borax," as Parker the composer affectionately called Dvorak, in tow I assured Mrs. Thurber that he would be safe in my hands, and then I proceeded to show him certain sections of our old town, chiefly the near east side. As he was a fervent Roman Catholic I found a Bohemian church for him; he invariably began his day by attending the first mass. Jauntily I invited him to taste the treacherous national drink called whisky cocktail. He nodded with that head which looked like an angry bulldog bearded. At first he scared me with his fierce Slavonic eyes, yet he was as mild-mannered a musical pirate as ever scuttled a pupil's counterpoint. I always thought of him as a boned-pirate. But I made a mistake in believing that American strong waters would upset his nerves. We began our rounds at Goerwitz's, then, as now, Scheffel Hall, which stood across the street from the National Conservatory. Later we went down to Gus Lüchow's; for a musician not to be seen at Lüchow's argued that he was unknown in the social world of tone. We traversed the great thirst belt of the neighborhood. At each stopping-place Doc Borax absorbed a cocktail or two. He seemed to take to them as a prohibitionist takes to personal abuse.

Now, alcohol I abhor. Therefore I stuck to my usual three-voiced invention of hops, malt, and water. We conversed in German, for he knew no English, and I rejoiced at meeting a man whose Teutonic accent, above all whose grammar, was worse than mine. Yet we got along swimmingly — an appropriate enough image, as the thirst-weather was wet, though not squally. He told me of his admiration for Brahms and of that composer's admiration for Dvorak. I agreed with Brahms. After he had put away about nineteen cocktails, maybe more, I said, rather thickly: "Master, don't you think it's time we ate something?" He gazed at me through those jungle whiskers, which met his tumbled hair half way. He grunted: "Eat! I no eat. We go to Houston Street. You go, hein! We drink the slivavitch. It makes warm after beer." I didn't go that evening to the East Houston Street café with Dr. Antonin Dvorak. I never went there with him, for I not only feared the slivavitch, but also that deadly Humoresque played by a fake gypsy fiddler, attired in a red coat and wearing an ineffable grin. Such a man as Old Borax was as dangerous to a moderate drinker as a false beacon to a shipwrecked sailor. His head was like iron. He could drink as much spirits as I could beer, and never turn a hair. I tell this anecdote, not for a moral purpose, but as one of the rapidly vanishing specimens of rum-lore, soon to become legendary. Next year the nation will be put in cotton-wool and its feeble will coddled by noble precepts and winning words from mouths smoking with fiery wisdom. And yet — it was a better time when Hammerstein smoked or Dvorak drank than the dusty prospect ahead for baffled thirsts.

ENRICO CARUSO

ENRICO CARUSO is dead. The enormous displacement caused by this lamentable happening is not alone confined to the artistic sphere but literally to the entire civilized world. We doubt if there are more than a half dozen public men on the globe to-day whose demise would so stir the universal imagination as has the passing of the incomparable tenor, for it must not be forgotten that the voice of Caruso has been heard, still is, and always will be listened to, from the equator to both poles, thanks to his vocal records, meagre, mechanical things, if you will, yet at least the simulacrum of his golden organ. It is a curious commentary on Théophile Gautier's famous poetic dictum that empires perish but art endures; that many of the great names contemporary with Caruso's will surely be forgotten, but the memory of his achievements not. Mankind always recalls with satisfaction the artists who have given pleasure to the senses. Kings are embalmed in deathless verse or live on the canvas of poet and painter. Yet where to-day are the monarchs who patronized Shakespeare, or Velasquez, or Molière? Their very titles would be forgotten were it not for art.

But actor and singer have not the luck of creative artists; they do but interpret, therefore, with their disappearance from the painted scene, for the majority there is naught but oblivion. The happy few who seem as of yesterday are, in the musical world: Patti, Rubinstein, Liszt, Rubini, Chopin — as pianist — Paganini, Malibran, and Lilli Lehmann. Great exemplars. To this brief list is now added Caruso. And he has one tremendous advantage over his celebrated predecessors — his voice is a living reality, after a fashion. That same voice has given profound satisfaction in hundreds of thousands of homes scattered over the world; that voice cheered the boys in the trenches during the World War. After all, it is a sort of immortality, this record, about as vital as we may hope for in a universe of changeless change.

Enrico Caruso is dead. There have been and will be other tenors, yet for this generation his memory is something sacred and apart. It is doubtful if the Metropolitan Opera House will again echo such golden music as made by his throat — that is, doubtful in our time. When he first came here, not two decades ago, there was a rich fruitiness to his tones that evoked such disparate images as the sound of a French horn and a golden autumnal sunset. Always the word golden comes to the lips. Golden, with a thrilling human fibre. Not the finished vocal artist that he developed into, nevertheless there was something indescribably fresh, luminous and youthful in the singing of the early Caruso. I had heard him in London before he sang here, which, alas! was to be his last home. Veteran as I was I could hardly trust my ears when he poured forth a golden stream of music, and with effortless art. It needed no critical clairvoyancy to predict that a star of the first magnitude had arisen in the firmament of art. That was in 1902, and since then this star grew in lustre and beauty till the day of his death. Caruso had not even then achieved his grand artistic climax. He was ever a prodigious student.

There will not be any critical dispute as to Caruso's place in the history of his art. Even in the brief span of life accorded the present writer Caruso looms formidably. Originally a lyric, he ended as a heroic tenor. His vocal range was extraordinary. In his repertory he demonstrated his catholicity. From Meyerbeer's Les Huguenots to Flotow's Marta, from Rigoletto to Pagliacci, there are few lyric works that he missed. La Forza del Destino was revived for him by Mr. Gatti-Casazza, and he could squander his extraordinary art on such a trifle as Mascagni's Lodoletta. But to all his undertakings he brought a refreshing sincerity and tonal beauty. It is not to be denied that he was happier in Italian than French music; his Rhadamès outshone his Faust. Nevertheless, he overcame the seemingly insuperable difficulties of a foreign style and diction, and his John of Leyden in Le Prophète and Eléazer in La Juive rank among his greatest achievements, not to mention his Samson. There was the note of the grand manner in the assumption of John and incomparable pathos in the delineation of Halévy's persecuted and vengeful old Hebrew. As an actor he grew amazingly the last decade of his artistic career. Compare his light-hearted, frivolous Duke in Rigoletto with the venerable Jew in La Juive. Then we realize how far intense study intelligently directed may carry a singer. It has often been a cause of critical wonderment why Caruso never sang the music of Richard Wagner. What a Lohengrin he would have been, what a Parsifal, yes, even a Tristan! He knew every note of these rôles. Once for my delectation he hummed the plaintive measures of the dying Tristan. Tears came to my eyes, so penetratingly sweet was his tone, so pathetic his phrasing.

I have heard tenors from Brignoli, so fat that he waddled, to the Spaniard Gayarré; from Italo Campanini to Masini, Nicolini and the stentorian Tamagno; no one of these boasted the luscious voice of Caruso. Some have out-pointed him in finesse, Bonci; Tamagno out-roared him; Jean de Reszke had more personal charm and artistic subtlety; there have been fierier Turridùs and more sympathetic Don Josés, but Caruso's natural voice was paved with lyric magic, it was positively torrential in its golden mellowness. When in his prime, full of verve and unaffected gaiety — think of L'Elisir d'Amore and Marta — he was unapproachable. There were many of us who would rather have been Caruso than ruler of these United States.

The social man in him was irresistible. Generous, overflowing with the joy of life, his sense of humor found one outlet in his caricatures — his pencil was clever as well as witty — and in the company of his friends. He was a good friend. No need here to speak of his ready response to those in trouble. He was exploited, of course, yet his belief in humanity was never shaken. An Italian patriot, he was also a lover of his adopted land. He was always a boy. He really never grew up. The eternal boy in him, mischievous, mirthful, coupled with his gift of mimicry, endeared him to every one. He fairly bubbled with kindly humor, and not the least among his many admirable traits was his conscientious attitude toward his audiences. Not to disappoint an expectant audience often cost him much personal suffering. He has sung when he should have been in bed with doctors and nurses. In Brooklyn he persisted in singing until a ruptured vein filled his throat with blood. The same desire, and not a craving for more fame or money, impelled him to make long and fatiguing trips in order that remote audiences might enjoy his matchless voice.

Like the majority of his countrymen, he was frugal in his habits, eating little and drinking less. He abused the use of tobacco, and because of his nervousness cigarettes were a seda-

VARIATIONS

"Hold your breath as you go through this book—touring the universe with a man who takes all of life in its everlasting fecundity and efflorescence for his theme."

—BENJAMIN DE CASSERES, in the *New York Herald*.

STEEPLEJACK

TWO VOLUMES. ILLUSTRATED

"Not only interesting because of its record of Mr. Huneker's career and philosophy, but because it gives an excellent idea of the developments in art, music, and literature, both in Europe and in America, during the last forty years."

—WILLIAM LYON PHELPS, Yale University.

BEDOUINS

Mary Garden; Debussy; Chopin or the Circus; Botticelli; Poe; Brahmsody; Anatole France; Mirbeau; Caruso on Wheels; Calico Cats; the Artistic Temperament; Idols and Ambergris; With the Supreme Sin; Grindstones; A Masque of Music, and The Vision Malefic.

"If there is ever a real culture in this country its roots will run in many directions; but historians will not dig very far before they run across the Huneker-root, not only because of its tremendous vitality and world-tentacles, but because of its stark individualism and militant sap. He is the greatest of patriots who raises the intellectual levels of his country; and James Huneker is therefore, to me, the greatest of living Americans."—*Musical America*.

IVORY APES AND PEACOCKS

"His critical tact is well-nigh infallible. . . . His position among writers on æsthetics is anomalous and incredible: no merchant traffics in his heart, yet he commands a large, an eager, an affectionate public. Is it because he is both vivid and acute, robust yet fine-fingered, tolerant yet unyielding, astringent yet tender—a mellow pessimist, a kindly cynic? Or is it rather because he is, primarily, a temperament—dynamic, contagious, lovable, inveterately alive—expressing itself through the most transparent of the arts?"

—LAWRENCE GILMAN, in *North American Review* (October, 1915).

UNICORNS

"The essays are short, full of a satisfying—and fascinating—crispness, both memorable and delightful. And they are full of fancy, too, of the gayest humor, the quickest appreciation, the gentlest sympathy, sometimes of an enchanting extravagance."
—*New York Times.*

MELOMANIACS

"It would be difficult to sum up 'Melomaniacs' in a phrase. Never did a book, in my opinion at any rate, exhibit greater contrasts, not, perhaps, of strength and weakness, but of clearness and obscurity."
—HAROLD E. GORST, in *London Saturday Review* (Dec. 8, 1906).

VISIONARIES

"In 'The Spiral Road' and in some of the other stories both fantasy and narrative may be compared with Hawthorne in his most unearthly moods. The younger man has read his Nietzsche and has cast off his heritage of simple morals. Hawthorne's Puritanism finds no echo in these modern souls, all sceptical, wavering, and unblessed. But Hawthorne's splendor of vision and his power of sympathy with a tormented mind do live again in the best of Mr. Huneker's stories."
—*London Academy* (Feb. 3, 1906).

ICONOCLASTS:
A Book of Dramatists

"His style is a little jerky, but it is one of those rare styles in which we are led to expect some significance, if not wit, in every sentence."
—G. K. CHESTERTON, in *London Daily News.*

MEZZOTINTS IN MODERN MUSIC

"Mr. Huneker is, in the best sense, a critic; he listens to the music and gives you his impressions as rapidly and in as few words as possible; or he sketches the composers in fine, broad, sweeping strokes with a magnificent disregard for unimportant details. And as Mr. Huneker is, as I have said, a powerful personality, a man of quick brain and an energetic imagination, a man of moods and temperament—a string that vibrates and sings in response to music—we get in these essays of his a distinctly original and very valuable contribution to the world's tiny musical literature."
—J. F. RUNCIMAN, in *London Saturday Review.*

What some distinguished writers have said of them:

Maurice Maeterlinck wrote, May 15, 1905: "Do you know that 'Iconoclasts' is the only book of high and universal critical worth that we have had for years—to be precise, since Georg Brandes. It is at once strong and fine, supple and firm, indulgent and sure."

And of "Ivory Apes and Peacocks" he said, among other things: "I have marvelled at the vigilance and clarity with which you follow and judge the new literary and artistic movements in all countries. I do not know of criticism more pure and sure than yours." (October, 1915.)

"The Mercure de France translated the other day from Scribner's one of the best studies which have been written on Stendhal for a long time, in which there was no evasion of the question of Stendhal's immorality. The author of that article, James Huneker, is, among foreign critics, the one best acquainted with French literature and the one who judges us with the greatest sympathy and with the most freedom. He has protested with force in numerous American journals against the campaign of defamation against France and he has easily proved that those who participate in it are ignorant and fanatical."—*"Promenades Littéraires"* (*Troisième Série*), *Remy de Gourmont*. (Translated by Burton Rascoe for the Chicago *Tribune*.)

Paul Bourget wrote, Lundi de Paques, 1909, of "Egoists": "I have browsed through the pages of your book and found that you touch in a sympathetic style on diverse problems, artistic and literary. In the case of Stendhal your catholicity of treatment is extremely rare and courageous."

Dr. Georg Brandes, the versatile and profound Danish critic, wrote: "I find your breadth of view and its expression more European than American; but the essential thing is that you are an artist to your very marrow."